Usborne

First Illustrated SCIENCE Dictionary

Usborne Quicklinks

There are some really good websites where children can watch animated explanations and do puzzles and games to support their understanding of science. We have selected the best sites and provided links to them from the Usborne Quicklinks Website.

To visit the recommended websites, go to Usborne Quicklinks at usborne.com/Quicklinks and enter the keywords: first science dictionary

Internet safety

Usborne Publishing is not responsible for the content of external websites. Children should be supervised online. Please follow the online safety guidelines at usborne.com/Quicklinks

Usborne

First Illustrated SCIENCE Dictionary

Sarah Khan

Designed by

Michael Hill and Karen Tomlins

Edited by Kirsteen Robson

Illustrated by Candice Whatmore

Science education consultant:
Helen Wilson MEd, BSc (hons), PGCE
Oxford Brookes University

Contents

What is science?

Science is about asking questions about how the world works and testing out ideas to see if they are right. This book divides science into six areas.

You can read a section to find out all about a subject, or use the word finder at the back of the book to look up words or topics.

Living things

This section tells you what animals, people and plants need to live and grow. It also looks at how living things fit into our world.

Materials

Here you'll find out about different types of things and how they can change.

Forces

In this section you can read about pushes and pulls and what they do.

Light, sound and electricity

Here you can find out what you need to know about light, sound and electricity.

Space

This section tells you what is in space and how scientists explore it.

Scientific investigations

Here you can find out how to do scientific tests and what to do with the information you collect.

Being alive

You can tell if something is alive by looking at what it does. All living things do the things shown on these pages.

Moving

All living things move. They can change position by themselves.

Animals move to find food and escape from danger.

Plants move by growing. Above ground they grow toward sunlight.

Below ground their roots grow toward water.

Being sensitive

Living things are sensitive to their surroundings. This means that they can tell what is happening around them.

Animals use senses such as sight, hearing and smell to find out what is happening around them.

Plants grow toward light and water. Some plants have leaves that move when they are touched.

Nutrition

Living things use food to get energy. This is called nutrition.

Animals eat to get energy.

Plants make their own food inside their leaves.

 Find out more about: animal senses (pages 14-15); how animals move and feed (pages 10-11 and 16-17)

Respiration

Living things release energy from food by respiration. Most living things need a gas called **oxygen** to help them respire.

Oxygen is in air. Plants take in air through their leaves.

People take in air through their noses and mouths.

Oxygen is in water, too. Fish take in water through their mouths.

Removing waste

All living things need to get rid of waste that is left over after nutrition and respiration. The waste can be solids, liquids or gases.

Trees send their waste to their leaves, which then fall off.

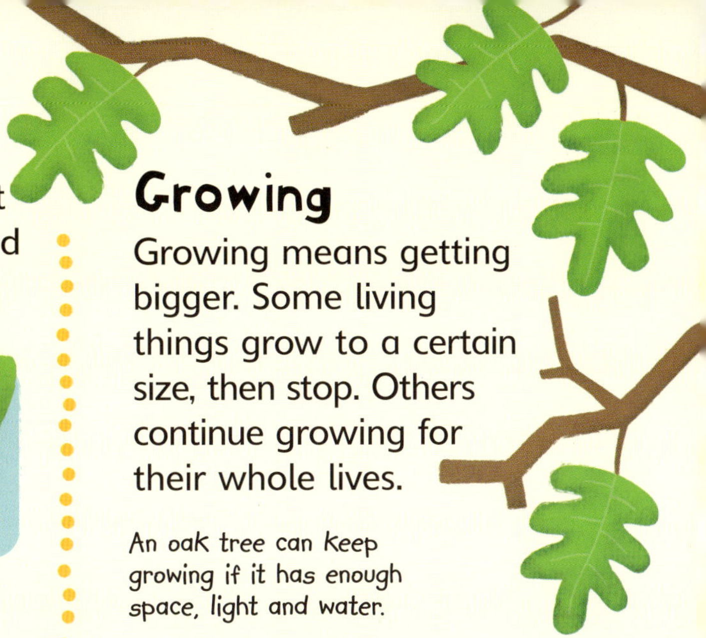

Growing

Growing means getting bigger. Some living things grow to a certain size, then stop. Others continue growing for their whole lives.

An oak tree can keep growing if it has enough space, light and water.

Baby lambs stop growing in size when they become adults.

Reproducing

All living things reproduce, which means they make new living things. If living things didn't reproduce, they would die out.

Adult ducks have ducklings, which grow up into ducks.

Find out more about: animal babies (page 22); how plants grow and reproduce (pages 28-31); solids, liquids and gases (page 51)

Cells

Living things are made up of living parts called cells. Some things are made of just one cell. Others contain millions of cells.

Cells are tiny, so you can only see them through a **microscope**. This is a special viewer that makes things look much bigger.

Tubes carry blood cells around the inside of your body.

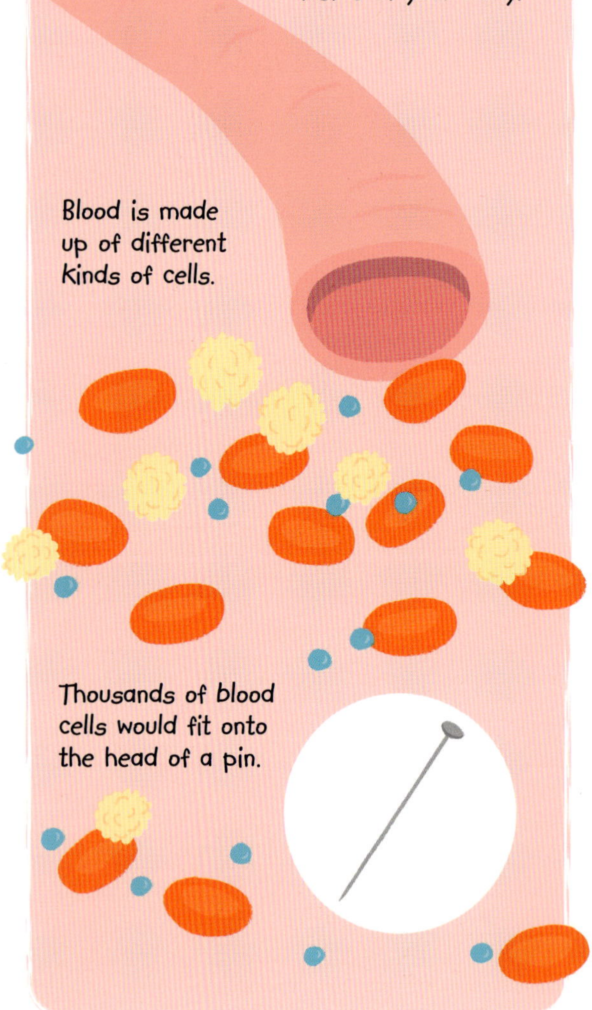

Blood is made up of different kinds of cells.

Thousands of blood cells would fit onto the head of a pin.

Living and non-living

Living things are made of cells and do all the things shown on pages 6 and 7. Something that does not do those things, or only does some of them, is described as non-living.

A bear is a living thing, but a teddy bear is a non-living thing.

Once alive

Some non-living things are made of parts that were once alive, but are not alive any more.

This tree is made of living cells and does all the things shown on pages 6 and 7. It is a living thing.

This fence is made of wood. The wood was once alive when it was part of a tree, but it is not alive any more.

 Find out more about: wood (page 46)

Never alive

Some non-living things are made of parts that have never been alive.

This toy duck is made of plastic. Plastic is non-living, so the duck was never alive.

This key is made of metal. Metal is non-living, so the key was never alive.

Non-living parts

A living thing can have some non-living parts. Some non-living parts were once alive, but others were never alive.

A snail's shell is a non-living part of its body. The shell was never alive.

A rhino's horn is a non-living part of its body. The horn is made of cells that were once alive.

Sorting living things

You can sort living things into different groups by looking at how they behave and what they look like.

Plants can be sorted into groups of plants that grow flowers and groups that don't.

Animals can be sorted into groups of animals that have a backbone and groups that don't.

Find out more about: flowers (page 25); metals (page 46); plastics (page 50)

On the move

People and animals need to move to find food, escape danger and keep healthy. The way they move depends on how their body parts, such as bones, joints and muscles, fit together inside their bodies.

Bones

Bones are hard parts that give a body its shape and help it to move. Different bones are joined together to make a frame called a **skeleton**.

This is what a person's skeleton looks like. It is made of 206 bones.

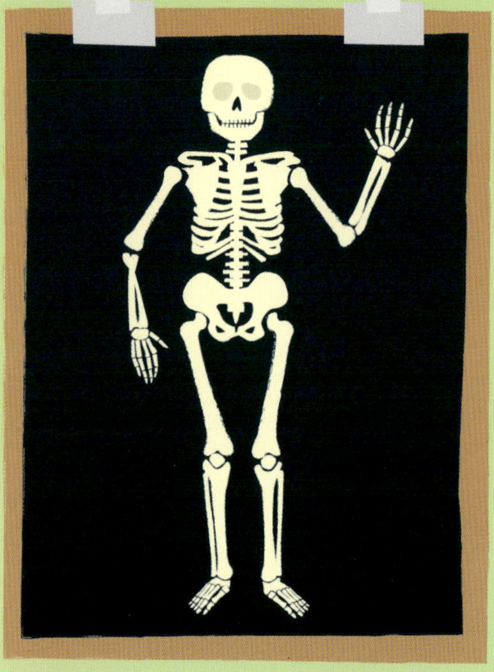

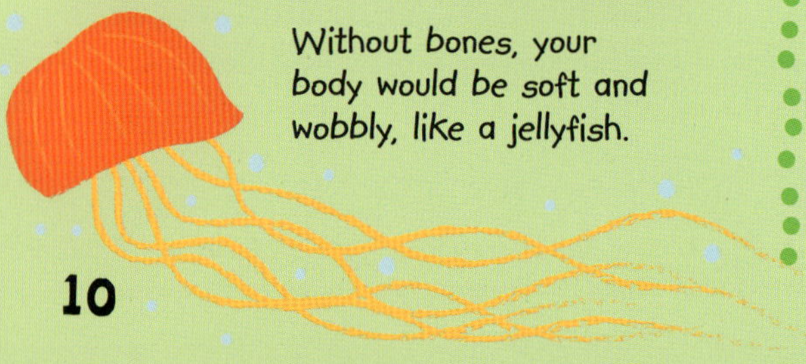

Without bones, your body would be soft and wobbly, like a jellyfish.

Different animals have different shaped skeletons.

This is what a hare's skeleton looks like.

Joints

A joint is a place where two bones meet. Without joints, an animal's skeleton would be stiff and wouldn't be able to move.

The joints in a hare's body help it to leap and run.

Muscles

Muscles are stretchy parts inside the body that help different parts of it to move.

You can control some of your muscles, such as the muscles in your arm.

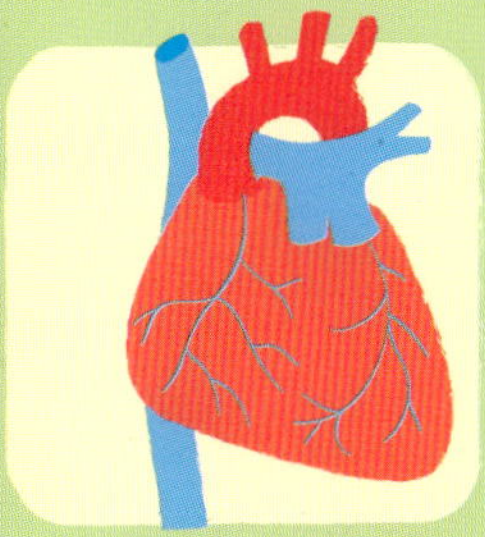

Other muscles, such as your heart, do their jobs without you thinking about them at all.

Fins

Fish have flaps called fins that stick out of their bodies. They use them to push themselves forward, change direction and stay balanced in the water.

The darker yellow areas on this fish are its fins.

Limbs

An animal's limbs are its arms and legs. Many animals use their limbs to walk, run or climb. Some animals crawl, swing or jump.

This orangutan is swinging through the trees using its arms and legs to move itself forward.

A crab uses some of its limbs to walk and others to fight off attackers and pick up food.

Wings

A wing is a part of an animal's body that can help it to fly. Birds and insects have wings. They move their wings to push themselves through the air.

Hummingbirds flap their wings quickly as they fly – around 50 times every second.

Find out more about: heart (page 19)

Body coverings

The outer layer of the body can be very useful. It keeps the body warm and dry, protects it from danger and helps it hide from enemies.

Skin

Skin is a layer that covers the outside of the body. It helps to stop harmful things, such as germs and the Sun's rays, from damaging the insides of the body.

Hippos have very thick skin – up to 12 times thicker than a person's skin.

Squid can change the color of their skin to hide from enemies.

Frogs don't need to drink water with their mouths – their skin lets in water.

Hair

Hair grows from the skin in thin strands.

Fur

Many animals have a thick layer of hair all over their bodies. This is called fur. Fur helps animals in different ways.

A polar bear's thick, white fur helps it to sneak up on the animals it hunts and also keeps it warm.

Cats make their fur stand on end so they look big and scary when facing an enemy.

Find out more about: germs (page 20)

Spines

Spines are sharp spikes that grow from the skin of some animals. Other animals don't try to eat spiny creatures because they don't want to be hurt by the spines.

A porcupine's spines usually lie flat. It raises them when it thinks it will be attacked.

Scales

Scaly animals are covered with small, hard flaps that protect the skin underneath.

A fish's scales overlap to make a protective layer, like tiles on a roof.

Shells

Animals that don't have any bones need something to protect their soft bodies. Many of these animals have a hard outer layer called a shell.

Snails are very slow so they can't run away from danger. Instead, they curl up inside their shells to hide.

A tortoise can pull its legs and head into its shell to hide from danger.

Many soft-bodied sea creatures live inside shells. When they die, the empty shells are washed up on beaches.

Find out more about: bones (page 10)

Senses

Animals find out about the world around them by using sight, smell, touch, hearing and taste. These are called senses.

Sight

An animal uses its sense of sight to find out what things look like. It sees things because light bounces off them and into its eyes.

Owls hunt at night. They have big eyes that let in as much light as possible, helping them to see in the dark.

Hearing

Hearing sounds lets animals pick up messages from each other. It also helps them find out where things are. Most animals hear sounds through their ears

Rabbits have long ears that can move in different directions to help them pick up even the smallest sounds around them.

Smell

An animal's sense of smell helps it find out if there is food, family or enemies nearby. Most animals detect smells through their nose.

Elephants move their long noses around to help them sniff out food and water.

Find out more about: seeing things (page 65)

Touch

An animal's sense of touch lets it find out what things feel like. For example, animals can feel if something is rough or smooth, hot or cold.

Often animals can sense touch better with some parts of their body than others.

Monkeys and apes explore new things by touching them with their fingers.

Cats use their whiskers to touch the edges of an opening, so they can tell whether or not they'll fit through.

Insects have sensitive feelers called **antennae** that stick out of the top of their heads.

Taste

When an animal tastes something, it is finding out whether it is good to eat. Rotten food and most things that are poisonous taste horrible, which puts animals off eating them.

Like this goat, most animals taste with their mouth and tongue.

Some insects, such as butterflies, taste with their feet so they walk over their food before eating it.

Find out more about:
eating (page 16)

Eating

Eating means taking in food to get energy. People and animals need energy to move around and keep healthy.

Food

Food is anything eaten that provides energy. Some animals eat only one kind of food, but others need different types to stay healthy.

Koalas eat only leaves from eucalyptus trees. They get sick if they eat anything else.

People need to eat lots of different types of foods. They get sick if they eat only one type.

Diet

An animal's diet is what it eats.

Some animals eat just plants. Others eat only meat. People, and some animals, can eat both plants and meat.

Rabbits eat only plants, such as hay, grass and vegetables.

Lions eat only meat. They hunt other animals for food.

People can eat lots of different types of plants and meats.

Mouths

To get energy from food, an animal first needs to turn it into a mushy liquid in its body. Chewing helps break up food.

Giraffes chew thorny leaves. Their lips and mouths are tough and hairy to stop them from getting hurt while they eat.

Teeth are used to chew and help break up food. Food is also softened with a clear juice called **saliva** that is made inside the mouth.

The inside of your mouth is wet because saliva is there to soften food. Teeth break food into small pieces.

Teeth

Teeth are hard parts inside the mouth that help break food into smaller pieces. There are different types of teeth that break food up in different ways.

Flat teeth help animals grind plants. Animals that eat plants, such as sheep, have flat teeth.

Sharp teeth help animals tear meat. Animals that eat meat, such as most sharks, have sharp teeth.

Find out more about: liquids (page 51)

Keeping healthy

To keep healthy, you need the right foods, enough activity and rest, regular checkups, and to stay clean and safe.

Playing sports can help keep you healthy.

Healthy eating

Healthy eating means eating things that your body needs. It is important to have different types of food.

Fruits, vegetables, beans and whole-grain bread are good for your body. Eating these foods will help you stay healthy.

Cakes, candy, cookies and chips are not good for your body. They have lots of sugar and fat in them. Eating too much of these foods will make you sick.

Sleeping

When you sleep, your eyes clos and your body relaxes. Your senses rest, so you can't tell what is happening around you as easily as when you're awak

Some people need more sleep than others. Most experts say that children need 10 or 11 hours' sleep a night.

If someone doesn't get enough sleep, they become tired, clumsy and grumpy...

...they find it difficult to think clearly, to concentrate, and to follow directions...

...and eventually they will become sick because their body and brain are not getting enough rest.

Find out more about: eating and food (page 16)

Exercise

When you exercise, you move around, which helps you stay healthy. Exercise is good for different parts of your body:

- **Muscles** – Exercise builds up your muscles. This gives your body power and strength.

Kicking a ball around can help to build up the muscles in your legs.

- **Joints** – When you exercise, you move your joints, which makes them stronger.

Dancing helps you exercise your joints, making them easier to move.

- **Lungs** – Your lungs are spongy parts inside your chest. They take in air when you breathe in, which helps to give you energy. Exercise makes you breathe deeply so your lungs get stronger.

Swimming helps to make your lungs stronger.

- **Heart** – Your heart is a big muscle inside your chest. It pumps blood around your body. (Blood delivers food to all the different parts and takes away waste.) Exercise makes your heart stronger.

Running makes your heart beat faster, which makes it stronger.

Find out more about: joints (page 10); muscles (page 11); waste (page 7)

Germs

Germs are tiny living things that can get inside another living thing and make it sick.

Germs are so small that you can only see them through a microscope.

This is a germ that causes colds. It can only be seen with a very powerful microscope.

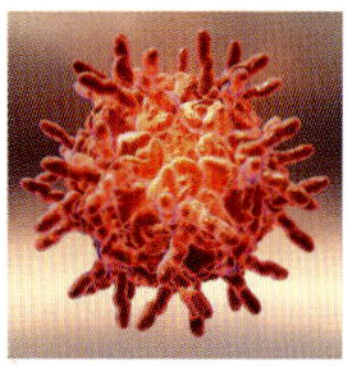

Being hygienic

Being hygienic means staying clean and safe so that you don't catch or spread germs.

Most germs are spread through the air in sneezes, coughs and even the air you breathe out. They can also spread in sweat, saliva and blood, and by touching.

Healthy habits

Having healthy habits means doing things to keep yourself and others healthy. Here are some ways to practice healthy habits.

Wash your hands regularly, especially after going to the bathroom, playing outside or before touching food.

Cover your mouth and nose with a tissue when you sneeze or cough. Use a tissue to wipe a runny nose. Put used tissues in the trash.

Brush your teeth in the morning and before you go to bed at night.

If you're sick, rest away from other people until you are completely better.

 Find out more about: microscopes (page 8); saliva and teeth (page 17)

Doctors

A doctor is someone who knows how to make you better when you get sick.

The doctor will talk to you and look at you closely to find out what's wrong, and how to make you better.

Sometimes people visit a doctor for a check-up, just to make sure that they are healthy.

Dentists

A dentist is someone who cares for teeth. It's important to have your teeth checked regularly by a dentist, even if they're not hurting.

A dentist looks at your teeth and gums, and fixes any problems.

Medicines

Medicine is something that you take to make you feel better when you are sick. A doctor tells you which medicine you need and how much to take.

Medicines are often syrups or pills and can come in bottles or packages.

Some medicines are a spray that you breathe in.

Skin medicines are usually creams or lotions.

Drugs

A drug is anything that people take to change the way their body works.

Medicines are types of drugs that can help people if they take the right dose. Taking too much medicine can harm or even kill you.

Life cycles

People and animals go through lots of changes in their lives. The changes that happen between being born and dying are called a life cycle.

Babies

A very young person or animal is called a baby. There are different names for babies of different animals.

A baby sheep is called a ***lamb****.*

A baby turtle is called a ***hatchling****.*

A baby bee is called a ***larva****.*

Eggs

Some animal mothers lay eggs Her baby forms inside the egg. When it has grown enough to live outside, it breaks out. This is called **hatching**.

These baby animals all hatch out of eggs.

Baby birds (called ***chicks****)*

Baby butterflies (called ***caterpillars****)*

Baby frogs (called ***tadpoles****)*

Birth

Some babies grow inside their mothers. When the babies are ready to live outside, they are pushed out. This is called birth.

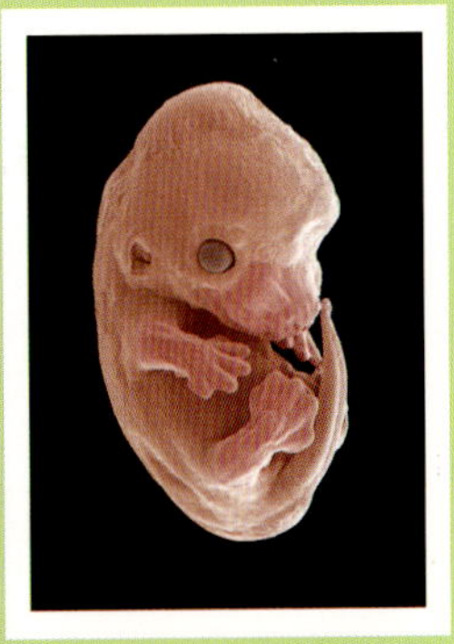

A baby mouse grows inside its mother for about three weeks before being born.

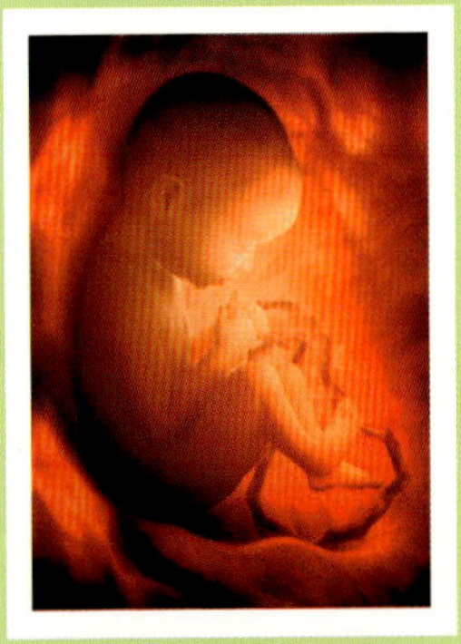

A human baby grows inside its mother for about nine months before being born.

Children

A child is a young boy or girl who is not an adult. Children learn how to do the things that adults can do.

Baby Child Adult

Adults

An adult is a person or animal that is fully grown and ready to have babies of its own. Different animals grow from babies to adults in different ways.

1. A tadpole gets bigger as it changes into a frog.
2. It grows legs, and loses its tail.

3. This is a fully grown adult frog.
4. Female frogs lay eggs with new tadpoles inside.

1. A caterpillar gets bigger as it changes into a butterfly.
2. It makes a case called a **chrysalis** around itself.

3. It breaks out of the chrysalis as an adult with wings.
4. Female butterflies lay eggs with new caterpillars inside.

Find out more about: wings (page 11)

Plants

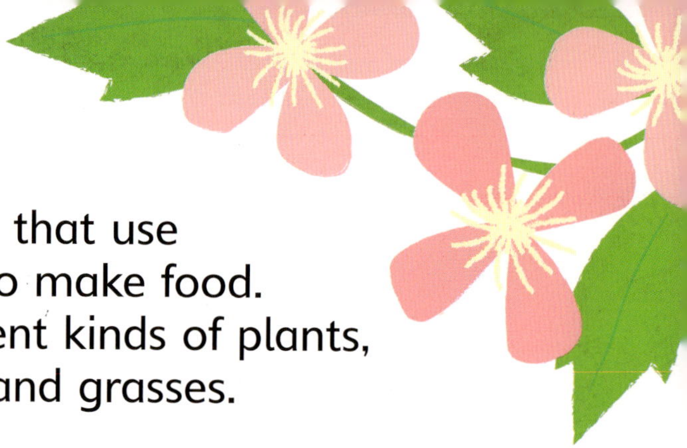

Plants are living things that use energy from sunlight to make food. There are many different kinds of plants, such as flowers, trees and grasses.

Parts of a plant

Most plants are made up of stems, flowers, leaves and roots. Each part has its own job to do to help the plant grow, stay healthy or make new plants.

Roots

A plant's roots usually grow underground to anchor the plant in the soil. Roots take in water from the soil, which helps the plant grow and stay healthy.

Most grasses have lots of thin, thread-like roots. The roots don't usually grow far down into the soil.

Many flowers have one main root that grows down into the soil, with some thinner roots spreading out from it.

Most trees have thick roots growing down and spreading out in the soil. Roots often spread wider than the tree is high.

 Find out more about: soil (page 47)

Stems

Stems hold up leaves and flowers, helping them grow toward the sunlight.

Stems help a plant's parts to reach sunlight, which they need to make food.

Stems also have tubes inside them that carry water and food to all the different parts of the plant.

Leaves

A plant's leaves are where it makes food, respires and gets rid of its waste.

Like this one, most leaves are green.

Flowers

Flowers make seeds, which grow into new plants.

The outer parts of flowers are **petals**. They are often bright colors and have a sweet smell.

The color and smell of petals often attract bees.

Flowers make tiny grains called **pollen** and other cells that are like tiny eggs. Seeds are made when cells from the pollen reach the egg-like cells.

A flower cut in half

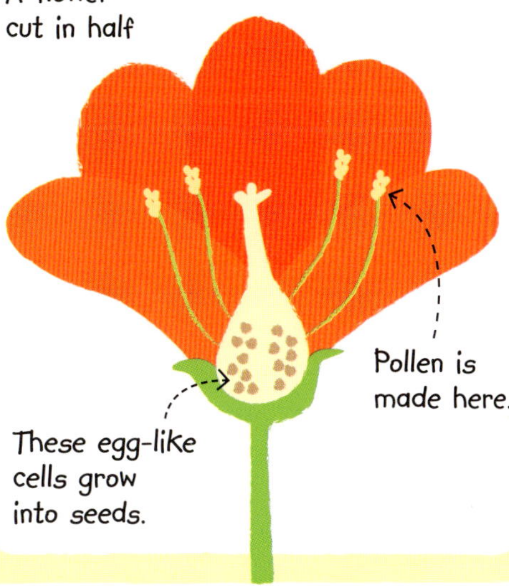

Find out more about: cells (page 8); food (page 16); removing waste (page 7); respiration (page 7); seeds (page 28)

Trees

A tree is a big plant that has one main stem made of wood. This stem splits into smaller stems called branches.

This oak tree has rough bark that isn't damaged easily.

Trunks

The trunk is the main, woody stem of a tree. Tubes inside the trunk carry water and food to the other parts of the tree.

The tubes join up to form rings, and a new ring grows every year.

This tree trunk has been cut across so you can see inside it. You can count the rings to find out how old a tree is.

Bark

A tree's bark is a hard layer that covers its trunk and branches, like skin.

Bark protects the insides of the tree from damage and diseases, and keeps them from freezing or drying out.

Beech trees have smooth bark that stops insects from climbing inside and damaging them.

Find out more about: skin (page 12); smooth (page 38); stems (page 25); wood (page 46)

Deciduous trees

Deciduous trees have leaves that lose their green color and fall off, usually in the fall. Fallen leaves have waste materials in them that the trees don't need.

In summer, this oak tree's branches are covered with green leaves.

By fall, the tree's waste is in the leaves, which change from green to brown.

By winter, the leaves have fallen off the tree. New leaves will start to grow in spring.

Evergreen trees

An evergreen tree loses a few leaves at a time, all through the year. This means that evergreen trees never have bare branches and always look green.

Evergreen trees look as green in winter...

...as they do in summer.

Find out more about: materials (page 38); removing waste (page 7)

How plants grow

Plants grow from seeds. For a seed to start growing, it needs water. Most seeds need to be buried in the ground too.

Fruit

A fruit is a part of a plant that has seeds inside.

When a flower's petals die and fall away, its inside parts grow into a fruit.

The insides of these raspberry flowers grow into raspberry fruits.

Seeds

A seed can grow into a plant. It has a tiny root, and a tiny stem and leaf called a **shoot**, inside it. It also has food inside. The food gives it the energy it needs to start growing.

A bean is a type of seed. This picture shows a bean that has been cut in half so you can see inside it.

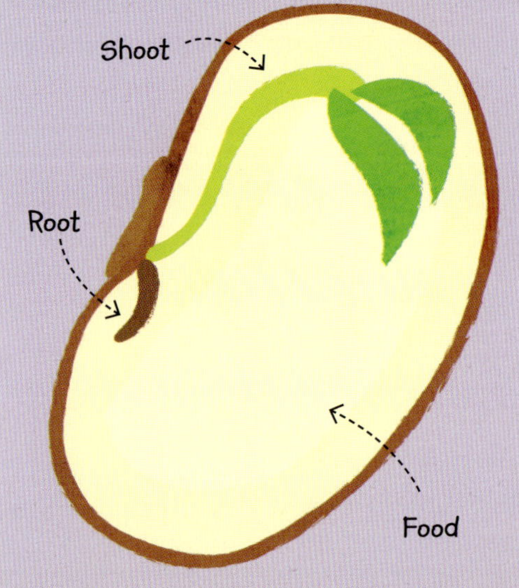

Find out more about: flowers, leaves and stems (page 25); roots (page 24)

Spreading seeds

It is better for seeds to move away from their parent plant before they start to grow. Plants spread their seeds in different ways.

- **By animals** – Seeds are often carried away from plants when fruits stick to animals' feet or fur, or animals eat fruits with the seeds inside.

The seeds inside this berry will come out in the bird's droppings.

- **By water** – Some plants that grow near water drop their fruit and seeds into the water. These float away and the seeds grow when they reach dry land.

Coconut fruits fall from trees, float away on the sea and are washed up on other beaches.

- **By wind** – Some plants have fruits that are very light and can be blown away by the wind. The seeds grow where the fruits land.

Dandelion fruits have hairs that catch the wind and carry the fruits away.

- **By explosion** – Some fruits have thin, firm cases. As the cases dry out in the sun and the seeds grow inside, the cases become tighter and tighter. They burst open, flinging the seeds out.

Pea pods burst open and hurl out their seeds.

Planting and watering

When you **plant** a seed, you make a hole in the ground (or in a pot of soil), put the seed in and cover it with soil.

Most seeds need to be in soil before they can grow.

Different seeds grow best at different temperatures. This pea seed should be planted in cool weather.

Seeds can't grow without water. They can get it from rain, but might need watering if the soil is too dry. **Watering** means sprinkling water on the place where a seed has been planted.

You can water a growing seed using a watering can.

Seedlings

A seedling is a baby plant.

Seeds grow into seedlings using food that is stored inside them. Once the leaves grow, they start making food for the plant.

When a pea is planted, it grows into a seedling.

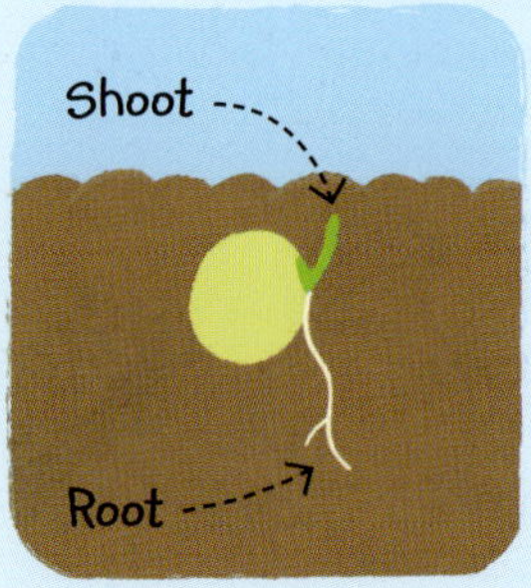

A pea in the soil grows a little root and a shoot.

The root grows down into the soil and the shoot grows up above the ground.

More roots grow and the shoot grows leaves. The plant is now a seedling.

 Find out more about: food (page 16); leaves (page 25); roots (page 24); soil (page 47); temperature (page 92)

Plants and light

Plants need light to be healthy. A plant growing in the dark is yellow instead of green and it can't make its own food. It grows quickly, trying to search for light.

This healthy cress plant has been growing in the light.

This unhealthy cress plant has been growing in the dark.

Find out more about: liquids (page 51)

Plant food

Plants take in goodness known as **nutrients** from the soil to help them grow.

Healthy soil has most of the nutrients plants need. Farmers often add extra nutrients to the soil to help their plants grow better. This is called **fertilizer**.

This trailer is spreading a type of fertilizer made from animal waste.

People can buy dry or liquid "plant food" to make garden and house plants grow better. This is a type of fertilizer.

When you water a plant, you can add "plant food" to the water.

Habitats

A habitat is the place where a plant or animal lives in the wild. Here you can see some types of habitats.

Woodlands

Woodlands are areas where lots of trees grow. There are often grassy spaces between the trees called **clearings**.

Animals and plants that like shade live under the trees. Those that like sunlight live in the clearings.

Fields

Fields are big open spaces where farmers grow crops, or keep animals such as cows or sheep. Fields often have hedges or fences around them.

Lots of different types of animals and insects live in fields or visit them.

Birds come to fields to feed on the plants and insects that live there.

Some animals, such as harvest mice, make their nests in fields, using the plants that grow there.

Ponds and lakes

A pond or lake is an area of still water with land all around it. Ponds are smaller than lakes and not as deep.

Wildlife comes to ponds and lakes to drink from them. Some animals, such as frogs and newts, lay eggs in the water.

 Find out more about: eggs (page 22); trees (page 26)

Streams and rivers

A stream is a flow of water that runs over the land. A river is a much larger stream that flows into the sea.

The water that flows in streams and rivers never changes direction.

Plants and animals that live in streams and rivers have to be able to cling on to rocks or swim against the direction of the water so they don't get washed away.

Salmon can swim against the flow of the water and can even swim up waterfalls.

Beaches

A beach is an area of land that is by a sea or ocean. The animals and plants that live there are used to being covered or splashed by salty sea water.

Many beaches are sandy.

Others are pebbly or rocky.

Some beaches are muddy.

Find out more about: oceans and seas (page 34); rocks and sand (page 47)

Seas and oceans

Seas and oceans are huge areas of salty water. Oceans are usually bigger than seas.

Oceans and seas cover most of the Earth's surface. They can be warm or cold, depending on where in the world they are.

The Arctic Ocean is the coldest ocean.

The Indian Ocean is warm. Many of the animals that live there, such as this reef shark, can only survive in warm water.

Mountains

Mountains are high, peaked areas that are bare and cold at the top. There are more plants and animals lower down a mountain, where it's warmer.

Evergreen trees and mountain animals, such as goats, live on the lower parts of mountains.

Deserts

Deserts are areas of land that are very dry. Fewer plants and animals can survive there than in most other places on the planet.

Many deserts are hot during the day...

...and very cold during the night.

Find out more about: evergreen trees (page 27)

Rainforests

Rainforests are large areas where trees grow closely together, and the weather is hot and rainy all year round. Rainforests are sometimes called **jungles.**

Rainforests have enough food, light and water for millions of types of animals and plants to live there.

Tundra

Tundra areas are covered in bare, sometimes rocky ground that is frozen all year round.

Only a few plants and animals (including polar bears) can survive in tundra areas.

Grasslands

Grasslands are vast, open areas covered with grasses, small plants and bushes. There are only a few trees.

Grasslands can be dry. There is enough rain for grass and a small number of trees to survive, but not enough for forests to grow.

Protecting our planet

Our planet can be harmed by some of the things people do. But there are ways to take care of our planet so that all living things have a clean and safe place to live.

Environment

The environment is made up of all the natural things around you. It includes the air you breathe, the ground you walk on and all the plants and animals.

Eco-friendly

Something that is described as eco-friendly is either good for the environment or does not harm it.

Planting trees is an eco-friendly thing to do. Trees take in gases that can be harmful and give out oxygen gas which people need to breathe.

Waste

Waste is anything that people don't need and so throw away.

Throwing away waste where you're not meant to is called **littering.** This can harm the environment and is against the law in many countries.

Animals can get trapped inside the litter left in their habitats.

Litter can also cut, choke or poison an animal that tries to eat it or find out what's inside.

 Find out more about: gases (page 51); habitats (page 32); planting (page 30); trees (pages 26-27)

The Earth is the only planet scientists know of where life can exist, so it's important to protect it.

Pollution

Pollution is any damage to the environment caused by things people do. Air, water and land can become polluted. Polluted places are dangerous to live in.

Oil being carried by ships can leak out and pollute the oceans.

Factories dumping their waste and people littering can pollute the land.

Smoke from factories, and exhaust fumes from cars and planes can pollute the air.

Recycling

Recycling is making new things from things that have already been used. This helps to make less waste.

Paper, cardboard, glass, metals and some types of plastic can all be taken to recycling centers and made into new things.

Earth's resources

Something useful is called a resource. Earth gives people lots of resources, such as rocks, wood, oil and water. Some of them are hard to replace, so it is important to find ways to save the Earth's resources.

Riding a bicycle instead of using a car is a good way to save the Earth's resources because it doesn't use gasoline (which is made from oil).

Find out more about: glass, paper (page 49); materials (page 38); plastics (page 50)

Exploring materials

Everything around you is made of stuff. In science, types of stuff are called materials.

Texture words

The texture of a material is what it feels like. Texture words include rough, smooth, soft and ridged.

Rough

Rough materials are covered in bumps or ridges.

Pinecones are rough and bumpy. Each bump is a protective covering for a seed.

Smooth

Smooth materials feel flat and even. They don't have bumps or ridges.

Marbles are smooth balls of glass. Being smooth helps them to roll easily.

Slippery

Slippery materials are difficult to hold firmly or to stand on. Smooth things can be slippery. Materials can also be slippery if they are wet or slimy.

Ice is slippery. If it wasn't, it would be easier to walk on, but more difficult to skate on.

Find out more about:
rolling (page 62); seeds (page 28)

Ridged

A ridged material has rows of long bumps or grooves on it. Ridged materials grip more easily than smooth ones.

The ridged rubber at the bottom of this boot can grip the ground. If it was smooth, the boot would slip.

Tractor tires have deep ridges that grip soft ground. If they were smooth, the tractor would skid.

Hard

Hard materials are tough and firm to touch. They can't easily be scratched, dented or squeezed into another shape.

This hammer's head is made from a hard metal.

If the hammer was soft, it would not knock in the nail.

Soft

Soft materials can be bent, scratched or squeezed. They are often gentle to the touch.

Soft materials are often used to make toys because children can play with them without hurting themselves.

These toys are made from soft fabrics that don't have any sharp edges.

Squishy

A squishy material can be pressed, squeezed or crushed. When this happens, the material changes shape.

A bouncy castle squishes when you jump on it because it is made from squishy plastic filled with air.

Find out more about: fabrics (page 50); grip (page 61); metals (page 46); plastics (page 50); pressing (page 58)

Appearance words

The appearance of a material is what it looks like. Shiny, dull and transparent are some words that can describe appearance.

Shiny

Shiny materials look bright. Light bounces off their surfaces really well because they are so smooth. They are often used to make things that need to look good.

Diamond stones can be cut and polished to make them very shiny.

Bicycle frames are sprayed with shiny paint to make them look good.

Metals are often shiny, such as this handle made from stainless steel.

Dull

Dull is the opposite of shiny. Dull surfaces don't look bright because they are less smooth so light bounces off less well.

Birds' eggs have dull shells. This helps them stay hidden from wild animals that might eat them.

Transparent

A transparent material is see-through. Light passes through it so you can see what is on the other side of it.

A magnifying glass is transparent, so you can see through it.

 Find out more about: metals (page 46); transparent (page 67)

Weight words

The weight of a material describes how easy it is to move or lift it. Heavy and light are words that describe weight.

Light

Light materials don't weigh much and are easier to move than heavy materials. They are often used for making things that people wear or hold.

This umbrella is made from a light material called nylon.

It is easy to hold it up in the air for a long time.

Heavy

Heavy materials weigh a lot and are difficult to move.

A heavy metal anchor can be tied to a boat and dropped to the bottom of the sea to stop the boat from floating away.

Strength words

The strength of a material describes how easy it is to break it. Strong and fragile are useful words for talking about strength.

Strong

Strong materials are tough, and don't break easily. They are used to make things that need to carry a lot of weight.

A forklift truck is made from strong metal, so it can lift heavy things.

Fragile

Fragile materials break or shatter easily.

This chocolate bar is easy to snap into pieces because it is fragile.

Find out more about: weight (pages 91-92)

How materials behave

You can describe a material by talking about what it can do or how it behaves.

Flexible

If a material is flexible, it means you can change its shape easily. If you can bend, squash, twist, squeeze or stretch a material, it is flexible.

Elastic hairbands are flexible because you can stretch and twist them.

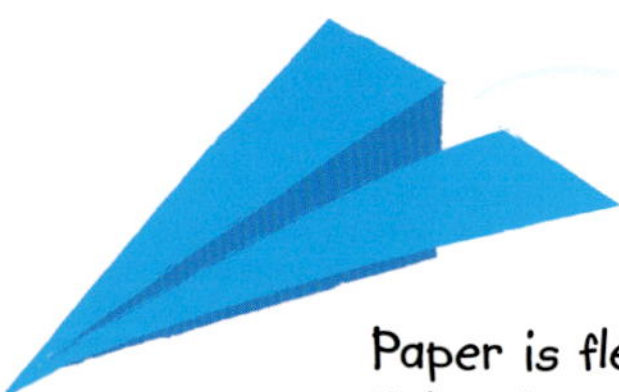

Paper is flexible because it bends and folds easily.

Bubble gum is flexible because it stretches when you blow into it.

Stretchy

A stretchy material is something flexible that you can pull into a new shape by making it longer or wider.

Some stretchy materials, such as dough, stay in their new shape once you stop pulling them.

Other stretchy materials, such as rubber, can go back to their old shape once you stop pulling them.

 Find out more about: bending and folding (page 53); pulling (page 59); twisting (page 54)

Rigid

A rigid material can't have its shape changed easily. If you can't squash, squeeze, bend, stretch or twist a material, it is rigid.

The frame of a chair needs to be rigid to hold a person without changing shape. It's made of rigid wood.

Waterproof

A material that is waterproof doesn't soak up any liquid or let any liquids pass through it.

This girl's coat and hat are made of waterproof plastic.

Rain doesn't go through the plastic, but rolls off it, keeping her dry.

Absorbent

An absorbent material soaks up and holds liquid easily. Absorbent materials are used to make sponges and cloths for cleaning.

Paper towels can absorb liquids.

Find out more about: liquids (page 51); paper (page 49); plastics (page 50); wood (page 46)

Floating

Something is floating when it stays on the surface of water. The water is pushing up on the object, stopping it from moving down to the bottom.

When you put something in water, it moves some of the water out of its way. An object can float if it weighs less than the water it moves.

Sinking

Something is sinking when it moves to the bottom of water. The water is pushing up on the object, but the push isn't strong enough to keep it on the surface.

When you put something in water, it moves some of the water out of its way. An object can sink if it weighs more than the water it moves.

 Find out more about: pushing (page 58), weight (page 91)

Magnetic

Magnetic materials are pulled toward magnets by a force called magnetism. All magnets and some metals, such as iron and nickel, are magnetic.

These objects all have iron in them. Iron is magnetic, so the objects are pulled toward the magnet.

Non-magnetic

Most metals and all other materials are non-magnetic. This means that they aren't pulled toward magnets.

Sand is non-magnetic.

Pieces of nickel are magnetic.

If you pass a magnet over a mixture of sand and nickel pieces, only the nickel will be pulled toward the magnet.

Poles

The ends of magnets are called poles. Magnetic forces are strongest there. One end is called the North pole, and the other is the South pole.

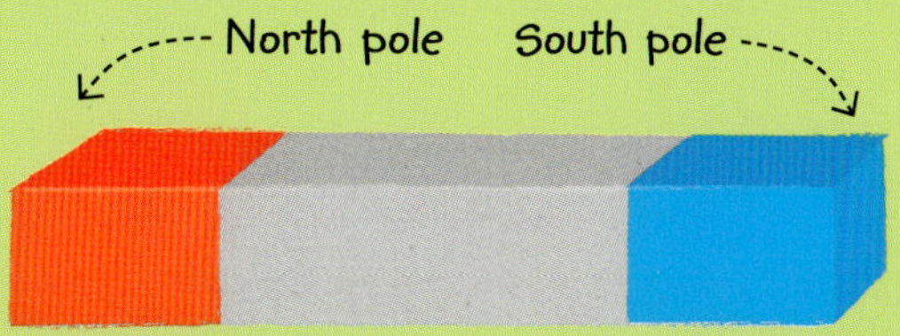

Attract and repel

When one thing is pulled towards another, it is being attracted to it. Magnetic poles of different types always attract each other.

The North and South poles of these magnets attract each other, so they pull toward each other.

When one thing is pushed away from another, it is being repelled by it. Magnetic poles of the same type always repel each other.

The two North poles of these magnets repel each other, so they push each other away.

Find out more about: forces (page 58); metals (page 46)

Natural materials

Natural materials are found in nature. People can grow them, dig them out of the ground or take them from living things.

Wood

Wood is a hard, strong material that comes from trees. It is used to make things that need to be tough and last a long time, such as furniture and houses.

This cabin is made from wood from the trees that grow in the forests where it was built.

Wood can be cut and carved using sharp tools to make it into different shapes.

This is a totem pole. It is carved from a tree trunk.

Metals

Most metals are shiny, hard and strong materials that come from rocks inside the Earth.

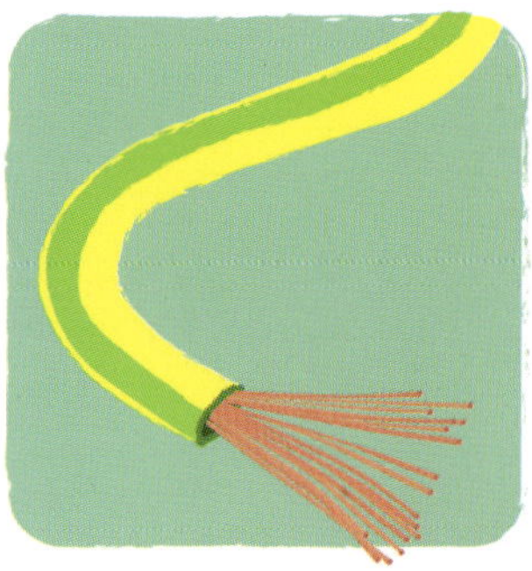

Copper is an orange metal. It is used for wires because it is flexible and good at conducting electricity.

Aluminum is a gray metal. It is used for making ladders because it is strong but light.

Gold and **silver** are rare and valuable. They are used to make watches and jewelry.

Find out more about: conducting electricity (page 77); flexible (page 42); trees (page 26)

Rocks

Rock is the natural material that makes up most of the surface of the Earth. Some rocks are soft and break up easily, but most are very hard.

Talc is a very soft rock. It can be crushed into a powder that can be used to keep things dry.

Diamonds are small, very hard rocks. They are shiny and rare, and are used to make jewelry.

Stones are small rocks. **Pebbles** are oval or round stones found on beaches and in rivers. They have been worn smooth by water and sand.

Soil

Soil is a mixture of tiny pieces of rock, dead plants and animals, water and air.

Trees and plants have roots that take in water from gaps in the soil.

Clay is a sticky soil that has very few air gaps in it.

Clay can be molded and dried to make pots.

Sand

Sand is made when sea waves break rocks and shells down into tiny grains. Sand is usually found on beaches.

The sand that is near the sea is wetter and stickier than the sand farther up the beach.

Find out more about: hard (page 39); roots (page 24); beaches (page 33); shiny (page 40); soft (page 39)

Wax

Wax is a material that is soft and sticky when it's warm, and hard and dry when it's cold. Some types of wax are made by plants or animals. Other waxes are man-made.

Bees make wax inside their bodies. They use it to build cells in their nests for storing pollen, food (honey) and their young.

Wax can be used to make candles and beauty products such as lip balms and hair gels.

Wool

Wool is the warm, fluffy material that grows on sheep. It can be used to make clothes and blankets.

The wool is cut off the sheep, cleaned, pressed and colored.

The wool is combed out into long strings which can be used to make cloth.

Cotton

Cotton grows as soft, fuzzy threads around the seeds of the cotton plant. The threads can be used to make clothes and bed linen.

Cotton threads protect the plant's seeds and help them blow away on the breeze.

The threads are collected, cleaned, colored and twisted into long strings to make into cloth.

 Find out more about: pollen (page 25); seeds (page 28); twisting (page 54)

Man-made materials

Man-made materials are not found in nature. They are new materials that people make from natural materials, to make them useful for different things.

Paper

Paper is made from wood. Small pieces of wood are ground up and mashed into a paste, then the paste is spread out into thin layers, pressed flat and dried.

Paper absorbs ink, so it is good for writing and printing on.

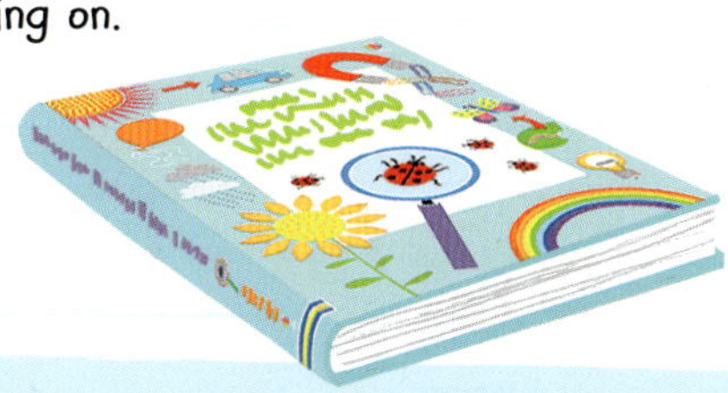

Cardboard

Cardboard is thick, stiff paper. It is soft and flexible enough to be cut and folded, so it is used to make boxes.

Cardboard is light and strong, so it is used to hold things that can be crushed easily, such as cereal.

Glass

Glass is a see-through material that is made by heating sand with a few other materials at a very high temperature.

Glass is see-through and doesn't have a color of its own, so it is used to make eyeglasses, windows and lightbulbs.

The front of this flashlight and the lightbulb inside it are made of glass.

Find out more about: absorbing (page 43); flexible (page 42); sand (page 47); wood (page 46)

Plastics

Plastics are light, waterproof materials that can be made into different shapes. There are many types of plastics, made in different ways.

These plastics are made by mixing man-made liquids with plant materials.

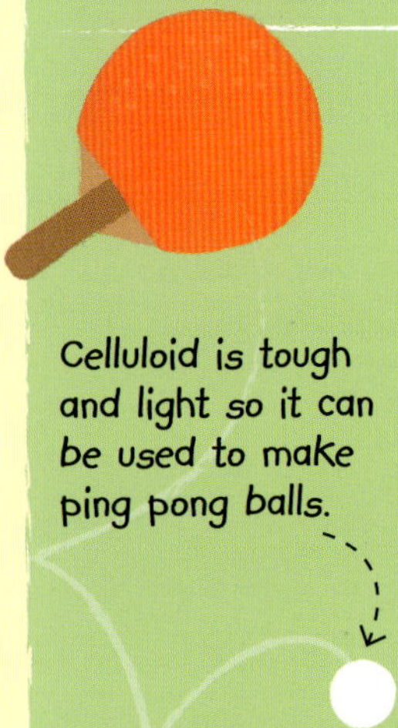

Celluloid is tough and light so it can be used to make ping pong balls.

Cellophane is see-through and flexible so it can be used as wrapping.

These plastics come from oil originally.

Acrylic is strong and doesn't scratch easily so it can be used to make cutting boards.

Polystyrene doesn't get hot easily, so it can be used to make cups for hot drinks.

Fabrics

Fabrics are flexible materials made of threads woven together. Some fabrics are made of natural materials (such as cotton or wool). Others are man-made.

Polyester is soft and dries quickly so it is used to make shower curtains.

Lycra is stretchy and quick to dry, so it is used to make clothes for dancing and playing sports in.

Nylon is light and strong, and doesn't let water through easily, so it is good for making tents.

 Find out more about: cotton (page 48); flexible (page 42); strong (page 41); wool (page 48)

Solids, liquids and gases

Materials can be sorted into three groups: solids, liquids or gases.

Solids

A solid keeps its shape unless something pushes, pulls, squeezes or stretches it. Solids don't flow or spread out easily.

Paper is solid. It keeps its shape...

...unless you push and pull on it...

...to make it into a new shape.

Liquids

A liquid doesn't have a firm shape. It can flow from one place to another and settles into the shape of the container it's in.

Juice is a liquid. It takes the shape of a pitcher.

When it is poured into a glass, it takes the shape of the glass.

Gases

A gas doesn't have its own shape. It spreads out in all directions to fill the shape of the container it is in. It can be squashed to take up less space.

When a gas such as air or helium is pumped into a balloon...

...it spreads out in all directions inside the balloon to blow it up.

There is enough helium squashed into this small tank to fill 30 party balloons.

Find out more about: paper (page 49); pulling (page 59); pushing (page 58)

Changing materials

Materials can change when you do different things to them. For example you can change the shape of some materials by squashing them.

Reversible changes

Some types of changes are reversible. This means that the change can be undone and the material can go back to how it was before.

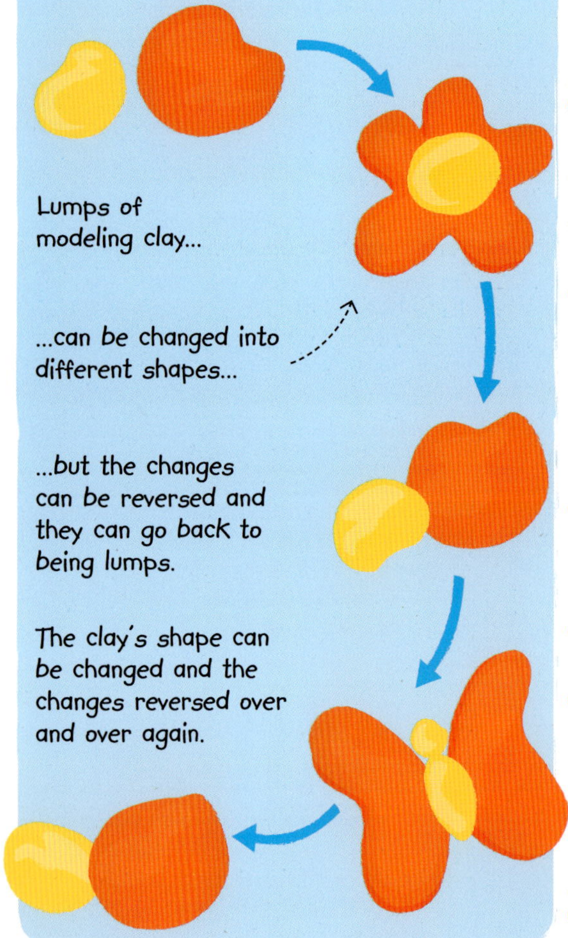

Lumps of modeling clay...

...can be changed into different shapes...

...but the changes can be reversed and they can go back to being lumps.

The clay's shape can be changed and the changes reversed over and over again.

Irreversible changes

Some types of changes are irreversible. This means that the change can't be undone and the material can't go back to how it was before.

Each stage of baking a cake is an irreversible change.

Once the ingredients are blended together, they can't go back to how they were before.

When the batter has been cooked in the oven, it can't go back to being the batter.

 Find out more about: cotton (page 48); plastics (page 50); pressing and pushing (page 58); pulling (page 59); stretching (page 42)

Bending

Bending a material means pushing or pulling it into a curved shape.

Squashing

Squashing a material means pressing or squeezing it to make it flat, soft, or out of shape.

Pillows and mattresses are comfortable to sleep on because they can be squashed.

Folding

Folding a material means bending it over on itself so that one part of it covers another.

When a material is folded, it stays in its new shape until a push or pull flattens it out again.

Twisting

Twisting something means holding it at both ends and turning it in opposite ways. It also means winding together strips by crossing them over each other.

Some materials are stronger when they are twisted.

Rope is made by twisting together long strands of plastic or fibers from plants.

By twisting the threads together, the rope becomes strong enough to hold a person.

Breaking

Fragile materials break easily, separating into pieces when a force acts on them.

The fragile shell of this egg has cracked after being tapped on a hard edge.

The shell breaks along the crack when it is pulled apart.

 Find out more about: forces (page 58); fragile (page 41); plastics (page 50)

Mixing

In science, mixing means jumbling up materials that can be separated back into their different material groups.

You can see the separate fruits in this fruit salad mixture.

Dissolving

When a solid dissolves, it mixes completely into a liquid.

Sugar dissolves in coffee. You can't see or feel the grains of sugar as you drink the coffee.

Separating

In science, dividing a mixture into its different materials is called separating. Separating is the opposite of mixing.

A mixture of pasta and water can be separated in a sieve.

The water falls through the sieve, and the pasta stays inside it.

Heating

Heating something means raising its temperature. Some materials change when they are heated.

If a wooden log is heated to a high enough temperature, it will catch fire.

The fire turns the wood to charcoal, smoke and ash.

Find out more about: liquids and solids (page 51); temperature (page 92); wood (page 46)

Cooling

Cooling something means lowering its temperature. Some materials change when they are cooled.

When liquid gelatin cools...

...it turns into a solid shape.

Freezing

When a liquid freezes, it turns into a solid. Its temperature drops so low that it can't flow, so it stays in one place and its shape becomes fixed.

When the temperature of liquid fruit juices drops low enough, they turn into a solid ice pop.

Melting

When a solid melts it turns into a liquid. As its temperature gets higher it loses its shape and starts to flow.

When the temperature of solid water (ice) rises high enough, it melts into liquid water.

When the temperature of solid butter rises, it melts into a liquid.

Evaporating

If a liquid is heated enough, it turns into a gas. This is called evaporating.

When you see puffs of steam, this is water vapor cooling down again to turn back into a liquid.

When water is heated it evaporates, turning into a gas called water vapor.

Find out more about: gases, liquids and solids (page 51); temperature (page 92)

The water cycle

The water on our planet is always moving between the sky, the earth and the sea. It can do this because it can change from one form to another. The way water moves around the planet is called the water cycle.

Exploring forces

A force is a push or a pull. You can't see forces but you can see what they do. Forces can make things start moving or stop moving, or change their shape.

Pushing

When you push something, you are using force to move it away from yourself.

The woman is pushing the shopping cart away from herself to make it move forward.

The harder you push something, the further and quicker it will move away from you.

This toy car only moves a little when it is pushed with a small force.

The car moves farther when it is pushed with a bigger force.

Pressing

Pressing something means putting a pushing force on it. When you press something, the force might move it, squeeze it or flatten it.

Pressing on a tube of toothpaste squeezes the tube and pushes the paste out.

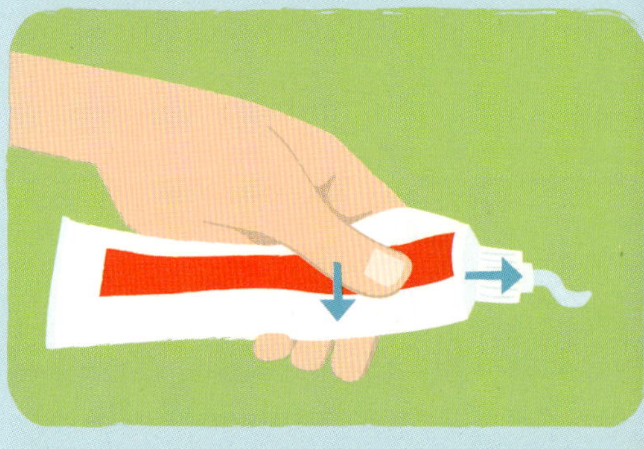

Pressing a rolling pin onto a ball of dough flattens it out. More dough is flattened as you roll it along while you press.

Pulling

When you pull something, you are using force to move it toward yourself.

This bird is using force to pull the worm out of the ground and toward itself.

Turning

When you turn something, you are pushing and pulling at the same time.

When you turn a doorknob, you push one way and pull the other to make the knob twist.

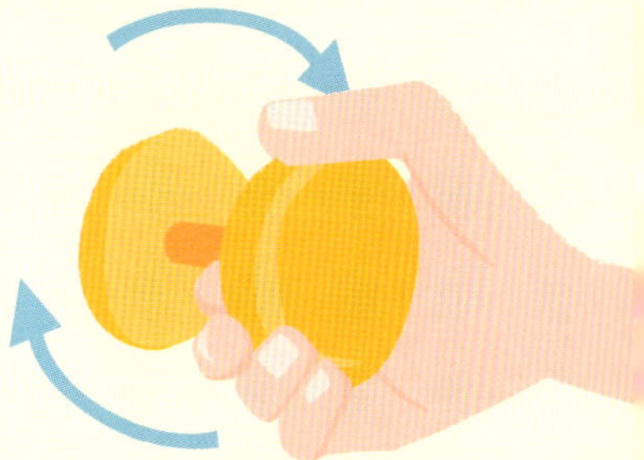

Starting force

Without forces, nothing would move. If something is completely still, it needs a force to start it moving.

It takes more force to start a heavy car moving than something lighter, such as a stroller.

Stopping force

Something that is moving will keep going until a force stops it.

Heavy things are more difficult to stop than light things. Fast things are more difficult to stop than slow things.

You can stop a marble that is moving slowly with just one finger...

...but you need both hands to stop a heavier ball that is moving very quickly.

Falling and rising

When something falls, it drops down. This is because there is a force called **gravity** that pulls everything down to the ground.

An apple falls from a tree because it is being pulled down by the force of gravity.

When something rises, there is a force lifting it that is stronger than the pull down caused by gravity.

An apple rises when you lift it because your upward pull is stronger than the pull down caused by gravity.

Direction

Direction is the path something takes as it moves. Things can move left or right, up or down, forward or backward.

A yo-yo can move in all directions.

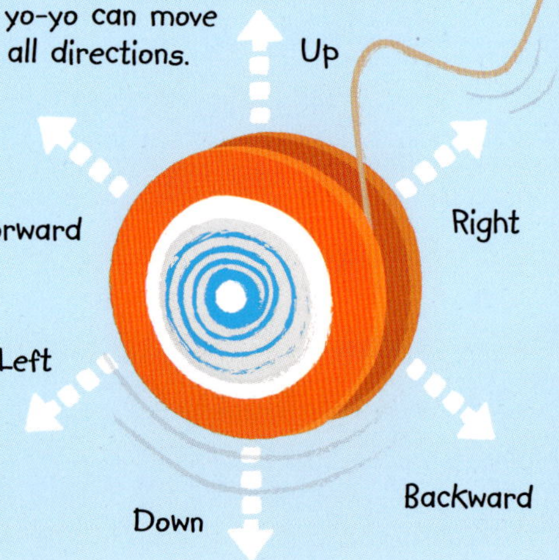

Changing direction

If something is moving in one direction, a force is needed to push or pull on it to make it change direction.

This basketball has been thrown upward...

...but it will change direction when another player pushes it down.

Surface

A surface is the outside or the upper part of something. You can find out how to describe what surfaces feel and look like on pages 38-40.

A wool rug has a fuzzy, rough surface.

Glass marbles have a smooth, shiny surface.

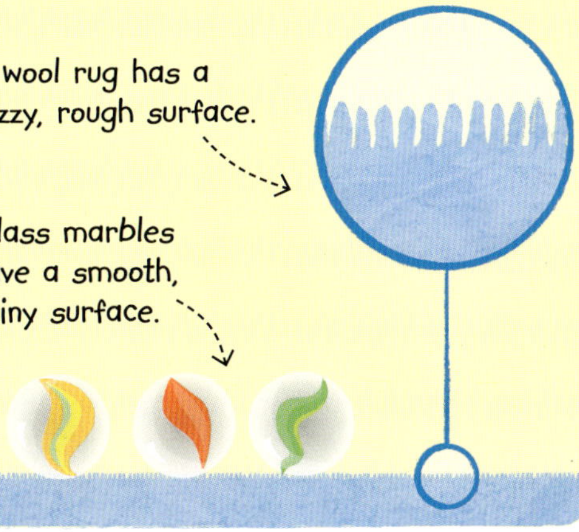

Grip

When a surface rubs against another surface and can't slide along it easily, it is described as having grip.

This racket's rubber handle has a good grip so it is easy to keep a firm hold of it.

Sliding

When something slides, it moves along a surface, touching it all the time. It takes less force for something to slide along a smooth surface than a rough one.

This plastic slide has a smooth surface, which makes it easy to slip down.

It is harder to slide down a wooden log because its surface is rough.

Oiling

If rough surfaces rub against each other too much, they wear away. Oiling something means putting oil between surfaces to separate them and stop them from wearing away too quickly.

When you oil a bicycle chain, a layer of oil stays between the moving parts that rub against each other.

Find out more about: glass (page 49); plastics (page 50); rough (page 38); shiny (page 40); smooth (page 38); wood (page 46); wool (page 48)

Rolling

When something rolls, it moves along a surface by turning over and over. It takes less force to roll something along a smooth surface than a rough one.

If you send a bowling ball rolling down a smooth bowling alley, it will go farther and quicker...

...than if you send it rolling along a rough surface such as tufty grass or a pebbly beach.

Speed

Speed is how quickly something is moving. The more force you use to start something moving, the faster it speeds up.

This row boat is speeding up slowly because the person rowing it is not making a big force.

This speedboat is speeding up quickly because the motor that powers it makes a big force.

You can work out how fast something is going by measuring how far it has moved and the time it has taken to move that distance.

Race cars can travel over 185 miles in an hour.

 Find out more about: measuring speed (page 94)

Gaining speed

When something is gaining speed it is getting faster as it moves. To make something speed up, a force is needed to push or pull on it.

Pushing on the ground with your foot will help you gain speed on a moving skateboard.

Losing speed

When something is losing speed it is getting slower as it moves. To make something slow down, a force is needed to push or pull on it.

Air is pushing on this bird's open wings, slowing it down as it lands.

Changing shape

When a force pushes or pulls on something, the force might change the object's shape.

Some things go back to their normal shape when the force stops pushing or pulling on it.

When you pull on a rubber band, it stretches and changes shape...

...but it goes back to its normal shape when the pulling stops.

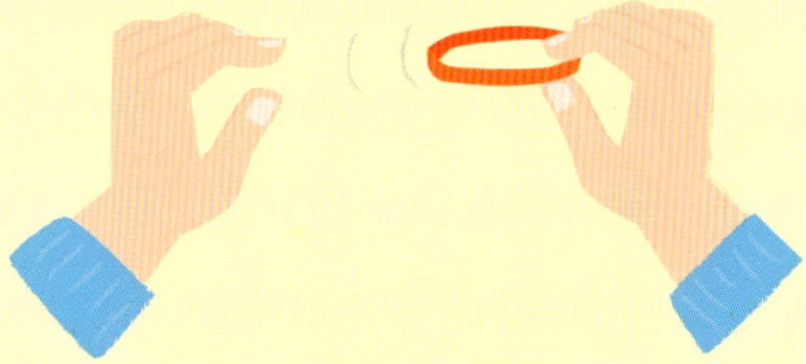

Other things stay in the new shape even when the force has stopped pushing or pulling on it.

A can changes shape when you squash it. It stays in this new shape even when the pressing stops.

Find out more about: stretchy materials (page 42)

Light

Light helps everyone see. Without it, everything would be dark, and nothing could live or grow.

Light sources

A light source is something that gives off light, often when it is heated or burned. The Sun is a natural light source. Other sources, such as candles, are man-made.

The Sun

The Sun is the closest star to the Earth. It is a big ball of flaming gas that gives off light.

On a clear, sunny day, there is lots of light.

Candles

A candle is a wax block with a string called a **wick** in the middle. When the wick burns, it heats the wax. Some wax turns into a gas, which gives off light as it burns.

When you blow out candles, their flames go out and they are not a source of light anymore.

Lightbulbs

A lightbulb is a glass case with wires or gases inside. Electricity flows into a bulb, heating the wir or gases, and making them glow.

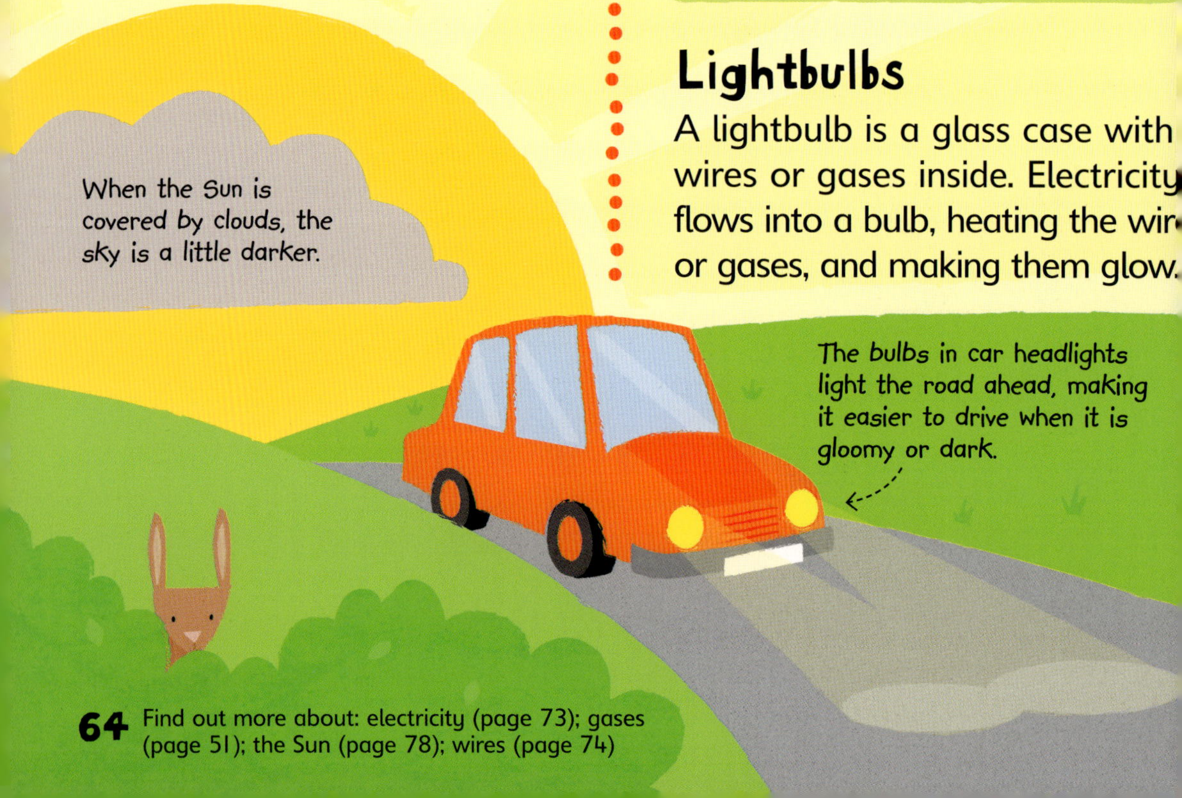

When the Sun is covered by clouds, the sky is a little darker.

The bulbs in car headlights light the road ahead, making it easier to drive when it is gloomy or dark.

 Find out more about: electricity (page 73); gases (page 51); the Sun (page 78); wires (page 74)

Dark, dim and bright

Dark things give off little or no light, or have little or no light shining on them.

With very little light in the room, it is dark. It is difficult to see much.

Something **dim** or **dull** gives off just a little light, or has just a little light shining on it.

When a lamp is switched on in the room, there is a dim light. You can see just a few things clearly.

Bright things give off a lot of light, or have a lot of light shining on them.

When more lights are switched on in the room, there is bright light. You can see everything clearly.

Seeing things

You can see things because light shines out from a light source, bounces off objects, and then enters your eyes.

Your eyes collect this light information and send it to your brain, which understands it as pictures.

Find out more about: sight (page 14)

Light rays

Light travels in straight lines, called rays. It doesn't curve around things. That's why you can't see around corners.

When you switch a flashlight on in the dark, you can see the light coming out in a straight beam.

Speed of light

Light moves faster than anything in the universe. It travels about 984,000,000 feet in one second.

The fastest manned spacecraft can travel over 36,000 feet in one second. Light is more than 27,000 times quicker than that.

Reflecting

Reflecting means bouncing off. Light reflects off things. Things that look dark and dull aren't reflecting as much light as things that look shiny and bright.

A shiny mirror reflects lots of light.

A dark sweater doesn't reflect as much light.

Things that reflect light aren't light sources because they do not make their own light. They are just reflecting light that has come from a light source.

The Moon reflects light from the Sun and doesn't make its own light, so it is not a light source.

 Find out more about: light sources (page 64); the Moon (page 79); shining (page 40); speed (page 62); the Sun (page 78)

Transparent

Transparent things are see-through. They let light pass right through them, so you can see clearly what is on the other side.

This glass goldfish bowl is transparent so you can look through its sides to see what's in it, and also what's behind it.

Shadows

A shadow is a dark shape where light doesn't shine. It is made when there's an object in the way of the light, blocking it.

The red flashlight on the opposite page is shining on the boy but the boy is blocking the rays. This creates a shadow of the boy on the wall.

Opaque

If something is not transparent, it is described as opaque. Opaque things don't let light through them, so you can't see what is on the other side.

The sides of this cardboard box are opaque, so you can't see through them.

You can use a flashlight and your hands to make shadow shapes on a wall.

White light

Most light that you can see, such as sunlight, is called white light. It looks colorless, but it is made up of seven colors of light.

When white light shines through a triangular glass block called a prism, the light splits into its seven colors.

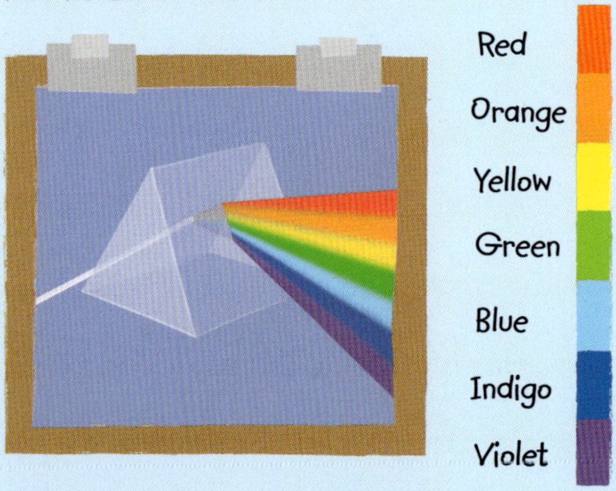

Rainbows

Rainbows happen when rays of sunlight hit tiny drops of water in the air. As the sunlight passes through the droplets it is split into different colors.

You most often see rainbows after a rain shower because there are more water droplets in the air.

Seeing colors

Things can take in and reflect different colors of light. What color you see depends on the colors of light that the object takes in and the colors of light it reflects.

Green things reflect green light and take in all the other colors of light.

White things reflect all the colors of light and don't take in any of them.

Black things take in all the colors of light and don't reflect any of them.

 Find out more about: reflecting (page 66)

Sound

Sound comes from anything that is making a noise. You hear sounds when they enter your ears.

Vibrations

Sounds are made when things vibrate. Vibrating means moving quickly backward and forward over and over again.

When you hit the bars of a toy xylophone, they vibrate.

The vibrating bars make the air vibrate.

The vibrating air goes into your ear. It makes your ear vibrate and you hear the sound.

When sound vibrations enter your ear, they move tiny bones inside your ear. Your brain understands the movements as noises.

How sound travels

Sound can travel through gases (such as the air), solids or liquids.

Many sounds, such as voices or traffic noise, travel to your ears through the air.

Sound travels fastest through solids, such as the string in this string and can telephone.

Sound can also travel through liquids, such as water.

If all the air is pumped out of this glass case, there will be nothing for the sound to travel through, so you won't hear the bell ringing.

Find out more about: gases, liquids and solids (page 51); hearing (page 14)

Loud and quiet sounds

Sounds can be loud, quiet or in between. How loud or quiet a sound is is called its **volume**.

A sound with a big volume is loud. A sound with a small volume is quiet.

Rustling leaves make a quiet sound.

A ringing alarm clock makes a loud sound.

Sound travels away from the source that made it. The farther a sound is from its source, the quieter it becomes.

If you stand next to a plane, its engine sounds very loud. The same plane's engine sounds much quieter when it is a long way away.

High and low sounds

Sounds can be high, low or in between. How high or low a sound is is called its **pitch**.

Something that vibrates slowly makes a low sound. Something that vibrates quickly makes a high sound.

A bird's throat vibrates quickly when it sings so it makes a high sound.

A cow's throat vibrates slowly when it moos so it makes a low sound.

Echo

Sounds can bounce off things. An echo happens when a sound bounces off something so you hear it again.

If you clap your hands in a big, empty room, you hear the sound right away.

The sound also bounces off the walls back to your ear, so you hear it again a little later.

 Find out more about: vibrating (page 69)

Vocal cords

Your vocal cords are muscles inside your throat. They vibrate to make sounds when you speak or sing.

If you put your fingers on the front of your throat and say something, you can feel your vocal cords vibrating.

Musical instruments

Musical instruments are things that make sounds when people make them vibrate. The sounds they make are used to make music. Each type of instrument makes sounds in its own way.

A drum makes a sound when you hit it.

A guitar makes a sound when you pluck its strings.

A recorder makes a sound when you blow down it.

Percussion instruments

A percussion instrument makes a sound when you hit or shake it.

These instruments make a sound when you hit them.

Triangle

Steel pan

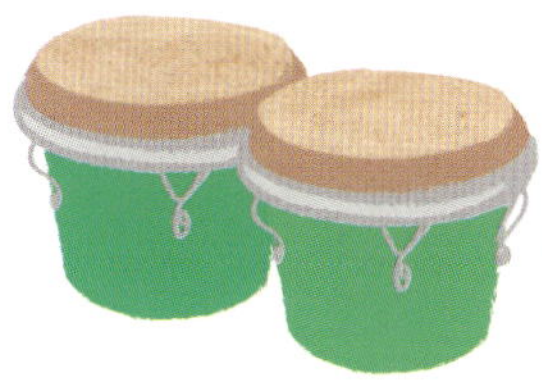

Bongo drums

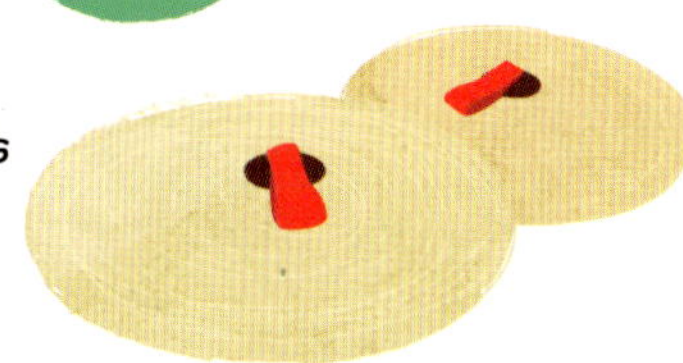

Cymbals

Xylophone

These instruments make a sound when you shake them.

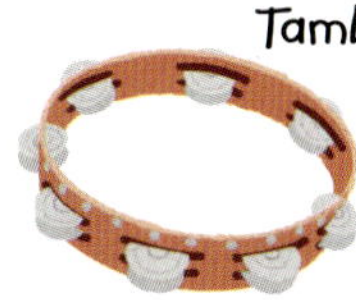

Tambourine

Maracas

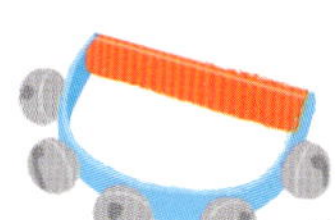

Bells

Find out more about: muscles (page 11)

Woodwind instruments

A woodwind instrument makes a sound when you blow into it.

Here are some woodwind instruments. When you blow into them, the air vibrates inside them and makes a sound.

String instruments

A string instrument makes a sound when you pluck or hit its strings, or slide a bow over them.

You slide a bow over the strings of a violin to make a sound.

You pluck the strings of a harp to make a sound.

Brass instruments

A brass instrument makes a sound when you blow into it.

You vibrate your lips against a cup-shaped mouthpiece. Air in the instrument vibrates and makes a sound.

Brass instruments are long metal tubes. As air flows through the tube, it vibrates and makes a sound. Here are some brass instruments.

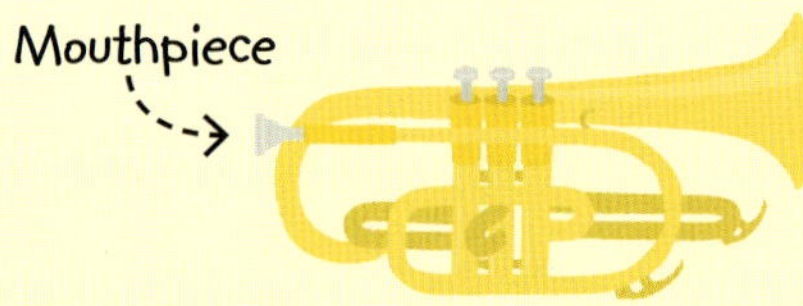

Cornet

 Find out more about: metals (page 46); vibrating (page 69)

Electricity

Electricity flows from one place to another. People use electricity to make all kinds of things work, from ovens and computers to lights and TVs.

Electrical appliances

An electrical appliance is a machine that uses electricity. Some appliances are plugged into an electrical socket. Others use electricity stored in batteries.

Lots of appliances need electricity to work.

Toasters, microwaves, ovens, refrigerators and freezers use electricity to heat or cool things.

Lamps, lights and street lights use electricity to make light.

TVs use electricity to make sounds and pictures.

Making electricity

Most of the electricity people use comes from big buildings called **power stations**. Inside a power station, huge fans called **turbines** spin around to make electricity.

The electricity flows along thick wires called **cables** or **power lines** to towns, cities and wherever else it is needed.

Pylons are huge metal towers that hold up power lines that run from power stations.

Find out more about: batteries, plugs and sockets, wires (page 74)

Electric current

Electric current is the flow of electricity.

Plugs and sockets

A plug is a connector on the end of an appliance's power cord. It has metal prongs that fit into holes in a socket built into a wall.

Electricity flows from an electricity supply through a socket and plug into the appliance.

Plugs and sockets look different in different countries.

In the UK, plugs and sockets often look like this.

This is what plugs and sockets look like in the USA and Canada.

In some European countries, plugs and sockets look like this.

Wires

A wire is a long, thin thread of metal that electricity can flow through. Wires are often covered with plastic to keep the electricity inside them.

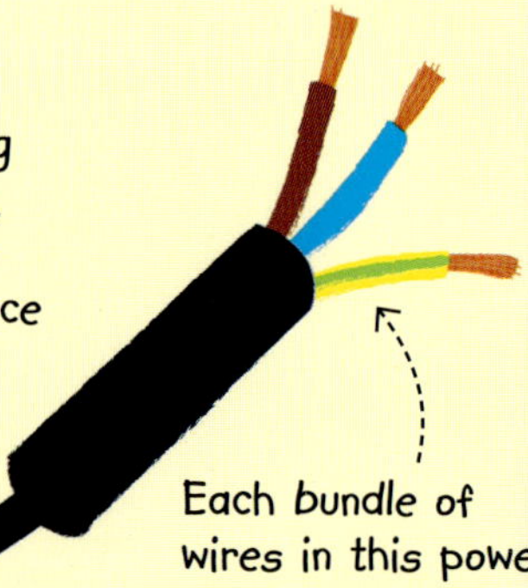

A **power cord** is a plastic covering with wires inside, that connects an electrical appliance to a plug.

Each bundle of wires in this powe cord is covered with plastic.

Batteries

A battery is a store of electricit that can be used to power things. There are lots of differe shapes and sizes of batteries.

Household batteries

Car battery

 Find out more about: electrical appliances (page 73), metals (page 46), plastics (page 50)

Circuits

An electrical circuit is a path that electricity can flow around. A circuit needs a power supply and something to join it together. You can add other parts to a circuit too, such as light bulbs and buzzers.

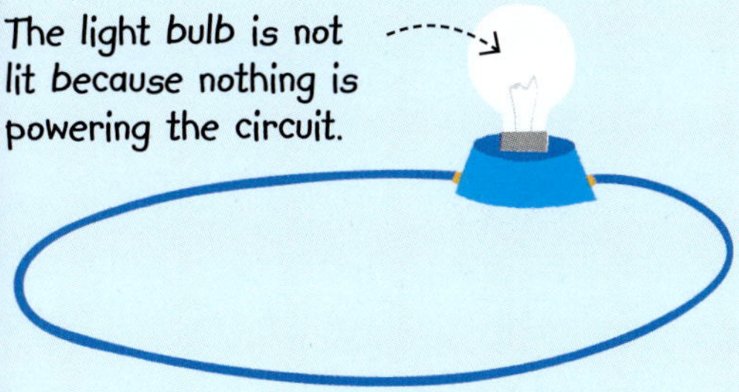

If a circuit has a gap in it, electricity can't flow.

Switches

A switch is part of a circuit that can be opened and closed to control the flow of electricity.

When the switch is 'Off', the circuit is broken. Electricity can't flow around it, so the bulb does not light up.

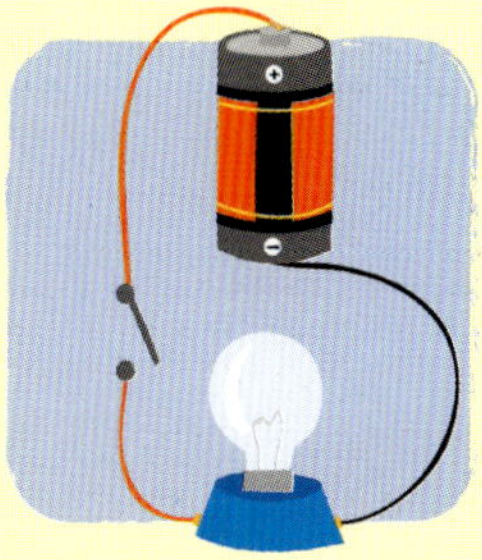

When the switch is 'On', the circuit is complete. Electricity can flow around it to light up the bulb.

The switch has been pressed down to complete the circuit and turn on the Christmas lights.

Find out more about: buzzers (page 76); light bulbs (page 64)

Components

Components are parts in an electrical circuit that do something when electricity flows through them.

- **Bulbs** light up when electricity passes through them.

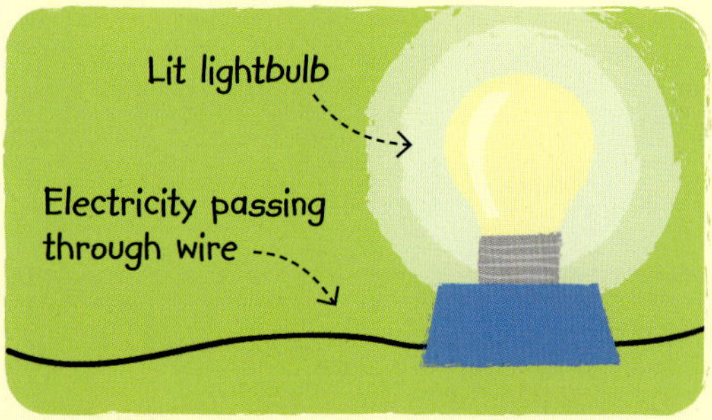

- **Buzzers** make a sound when electricity passes through them.

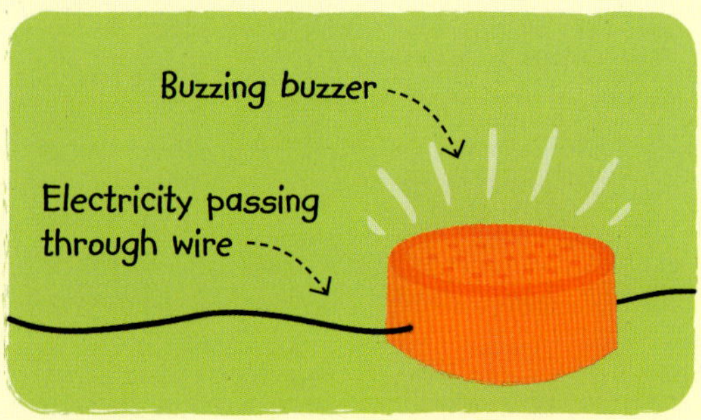

- **Motors** move when electricity passes through them.

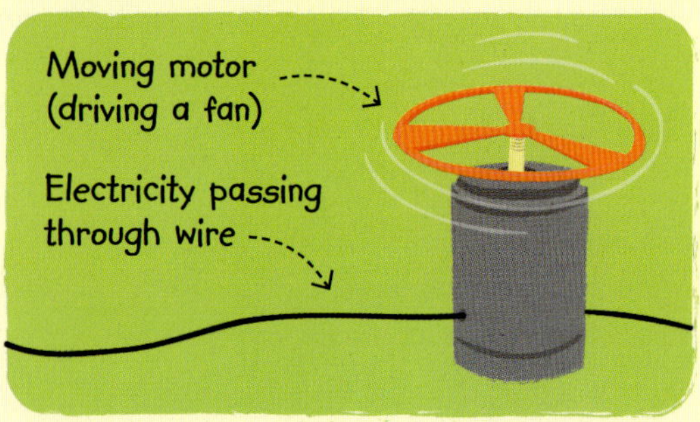

Leads

Leads are lengths of plastic-covered electrical wire with metal connectors at the ends. They complete circuits by connecting components to a power source, such as a battery.

These leads have connectors called **crocodile clips**. They can clip onto a switch to complete the circuit.

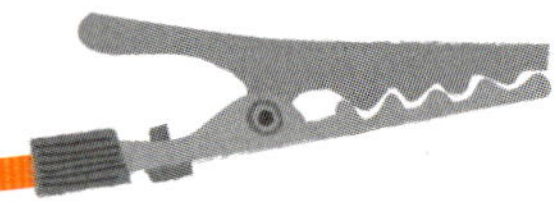

Electrical insulators

Electrical insulators are materials that don't let electricity through them easily. Plastic, glass and wood are good electrical insulators.

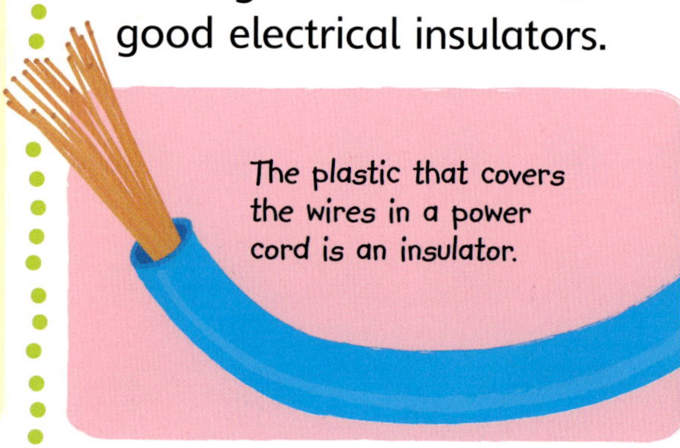

 Find out more about: batteries (page 74); electrical circuits (page 75); glass (page 49); lightbulbs (page 64); metals (page 46); plastics (page 50); wires (page 74); wood (page 46)

Electrical conductors

Some materials let electricity pass through them easily. They are known as electrical conductors. Metals are good electrical conductors.

Lightning is an example of electricity found in nature.

This charger has a metal part that fits into the tablet computer. Electricity flows through the metal into the tablet to charge it.

Many tall buildings have a metal pole called a lightning rod on top.

Lightning flows through the rod and down a metal ribbon to the ground, safely away from the building.

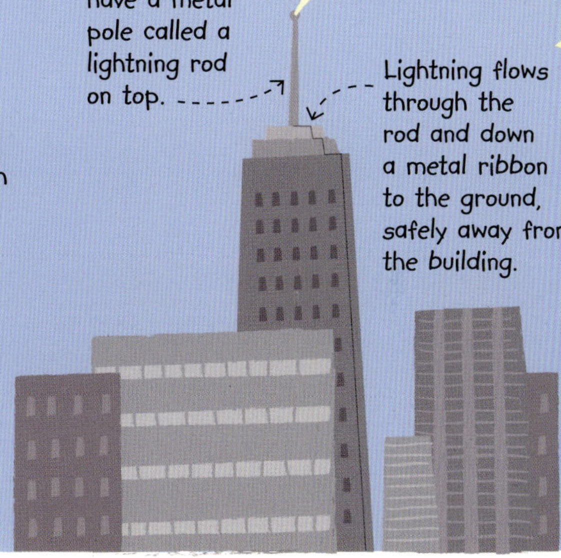

Electric shocks

An electric shock is a burn caused by electricity. Electric shocks can kill you. Electricity is dangerous to living creatures because the water inside their bodies is a good electrical conductor.

This sign is a warning that shows there are electrical machines or equipment nearby.

Electrical safety

- Never use electrical appliances near water.
- Never touch switches with wet hands.
- Always hold a plug by its plastic part.
- Never stick anything into a plug socket except a plug.

Find out more about: electrical appliances (page 73); materials (page 38); plugs and sockets (page 74)

Our Universe

The Universe is the name for space and everything in it. Most of the Universe is made up of empty space. Here you can see some of the other things in the Universe.

Stars

A star is a giant ball of flaming gas. Stars blaze for billions of years, giving off light and heat.

The Sun

The Sun is the closest star to our planet, and the only star you can see in the day. Without heat and light from the Sun, there would be no life on Earth.

Solar systems

A solar system is a star and all the planets and big lumps of metal, rock and ice that circle around it.

Planets

A planet is a massive ball-shaped object that moves in circles around a star. In our solar system, there are eight planets circling around the Sun.

These are the planets in our solar system.

This picture doesn't show exactly how much bigger the Sun is than the planets. In real life, the Sun is so big that you could fit more than one million Earths inside it.

The Earth

The Earth is the planet we live on. It is the third closest planet to the Sun, and it is the only planet we know where people, animals and plants live.

This is what the Earth looks like from space. The white areas are clouds and ice. The blue areas are seas and oceans. The green and pale brown areas are land.

The Earth is a huge ball of rock and metal. We live on its hard surface. Inside the planet it is so hot that some of the rock and metal there has melted.

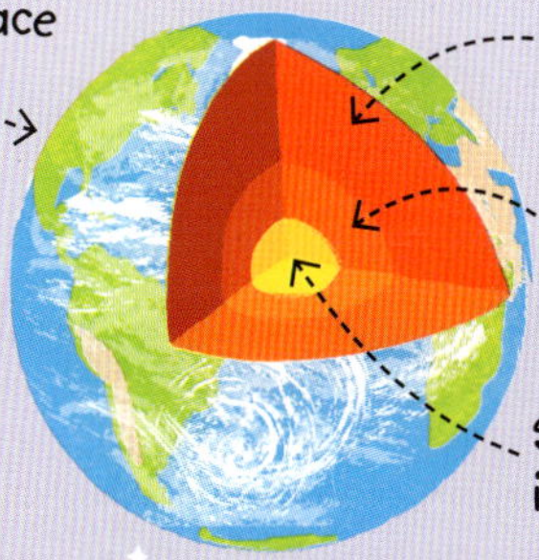

Moons

A moon is a huge lump of rock that circles around a planet in space. Most moons are rounded. A planet can have more than one moon.

The planet Mars has two moons, called Phobos and Deimos.

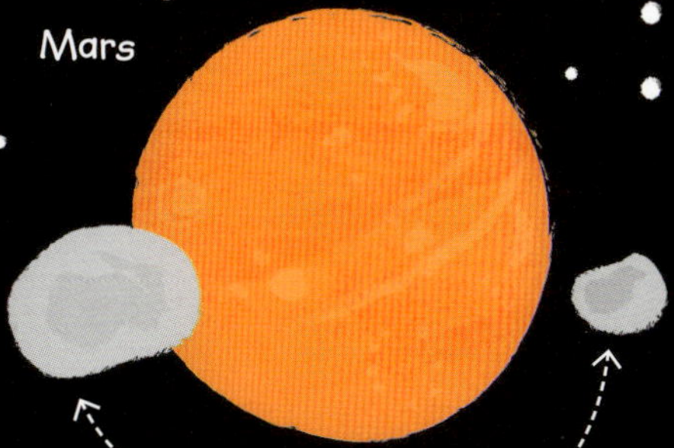

The Earth has one moon. It is a dusty ball of rock, a quarter of the size of the Earth. So far, the Moon is the only part of our solar system that people have visited.

Find out more about: metals (page 46); rocks (page 47)

Meteoroids

Meteoroids are pieces of rock that travel through space around the Sun. The smallest meteoroids are tiny grains. The biggest are huge boulders.

Most meteoroids are as small as a pebble, but the biggest are the size of a car.

Meteors

A meteor is a meteoroid that is falling toward the Earth. Small meteors burn up before they land on Earth. As they burn, they glow brightly. Meteors are also called shooting stars.

The brightest meteors are known as fireballs.

Meteorites

Meteorites are meteors that land on the Earth's surface.

The biggest meteorites leave massive holes, called ***craters****, in the Earth's surface where they land.*

Asteroids

Asteroids are big lumps of rock or metal that travel through space around the Sun. They are too big to be meteoroids but too small to be planets.

Most asteroids in our solar system are between the planets Mars and Jupiter, in an area called the Asteroid Belt.

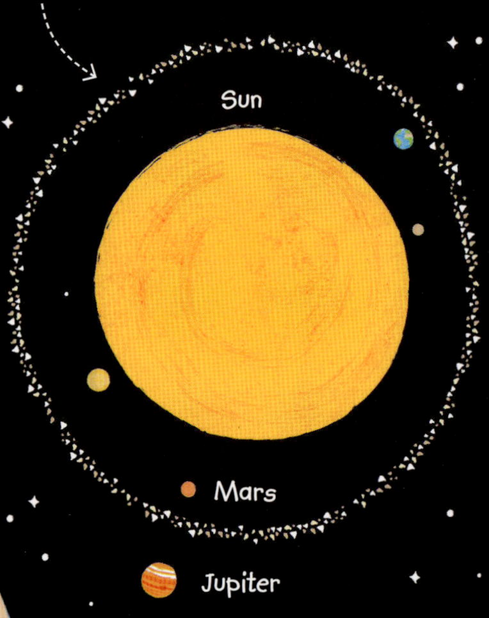

Comets

Comets are lumps of ice, dust and grit that travel around the Sun. As a comet nears the Sun, some of its ice melts. It releases gases and dust that stream out like a tail behind it.

Comets sometimes get close enough to the Earth for us to see them as a bright whoosh in the night sky.

A comet named Halley's Comet can be seen from Earth every 75 to 76 years. The last time it came close enough for people to see it was in 1986.

Orbiting

Orbiting means moving around something. Planets, meteors, asteroids and comets orbit the Sun. Moons orbit planets.

Find out more about: gases (page 51); ice (page 57)

Exploring space

You can look at space just by gazing up at the night sky. But, by using special equipment, people can see farther into space and a few people even go there themselves.

Astronomers

Astronomers are scientists who study space.

Many astronomers also teach at universities or colleges. Others help governments and companies plan missions into space.

An Italian astronomer named Galileo Galilei lived around 400 years ago. He made his own telescope and used it to discover many new moons and stars.

Telescopes

A telescope is a piece of equipment that makes objects that are far away look closer. Telescopes can help people see into space.

Some telescopes are small enough to use pointing out of a bedroom window.

Others are huge dishes that pick up signals given off by things in space, and turn them into pictures on a computer.

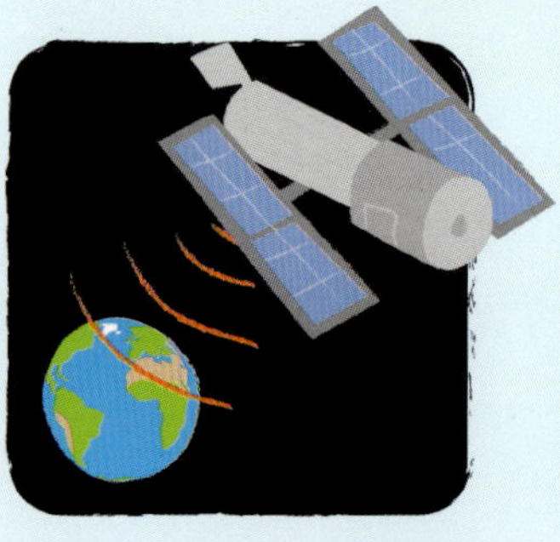

The most powerful telescopes are up in space, sending back pictures to astronomers on Earth.

 Find out more about: equipment (page 88); moons (page 79); stars (page 78)

Spacecraft

A spacecraft is a machine that carries people or things into space.

Spacecraft are attached to **rockets**. These have powerful engines which give the craft enough of a push to lift them off the ground, up into space.

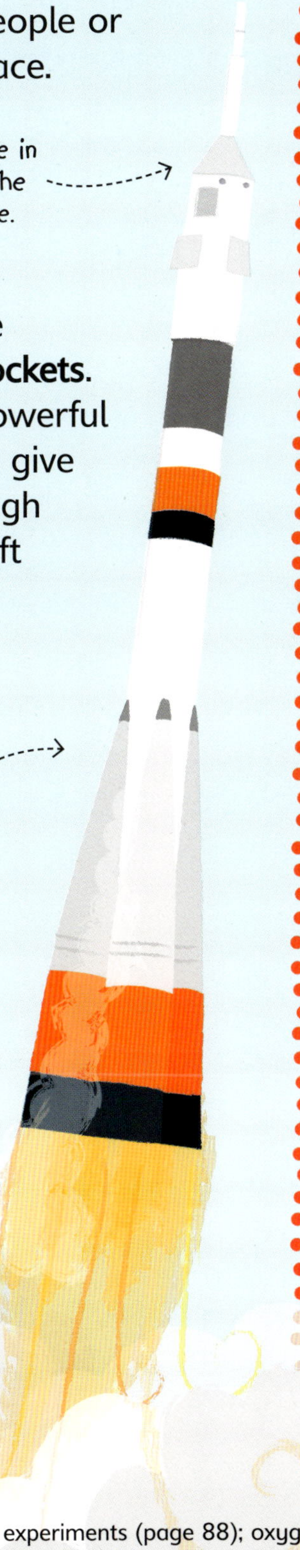

Astronauts

An astronaut is a person who has been trained to travel into space. In space, astronauts fly their spacecraft, do scientific experiments, and study planets and moons.

Space stations

A space station is a big building in space where scientists can live and do experiments. Scientists can live on a station for several years at a time.

Find out more about: experiments (page 88); oxygen (page 7); push (page 58); speed (page 62)

The Earth and the Sun

The Sun is the closest star to Earth. Without its heat and light, life on Earth couldn't exist. People also use the Sun to help them measure time.

Years

A year is the time it takes for a planet to travel around the Sun. On Earth, a year is just over 365 days long.

Mercury is the closest planet to the Sun. It takes Mercury only 88 days to orbit the Sun once.

Night and day

The Earth spins around, like a spinning top. It takes 24 hours to spin all the way around.

When one side of the Earth is facing the Sun, the sky is light and it is **daytime** there. The other side is turned away from the Sun. The sky is dark and it is **nighttime** there.

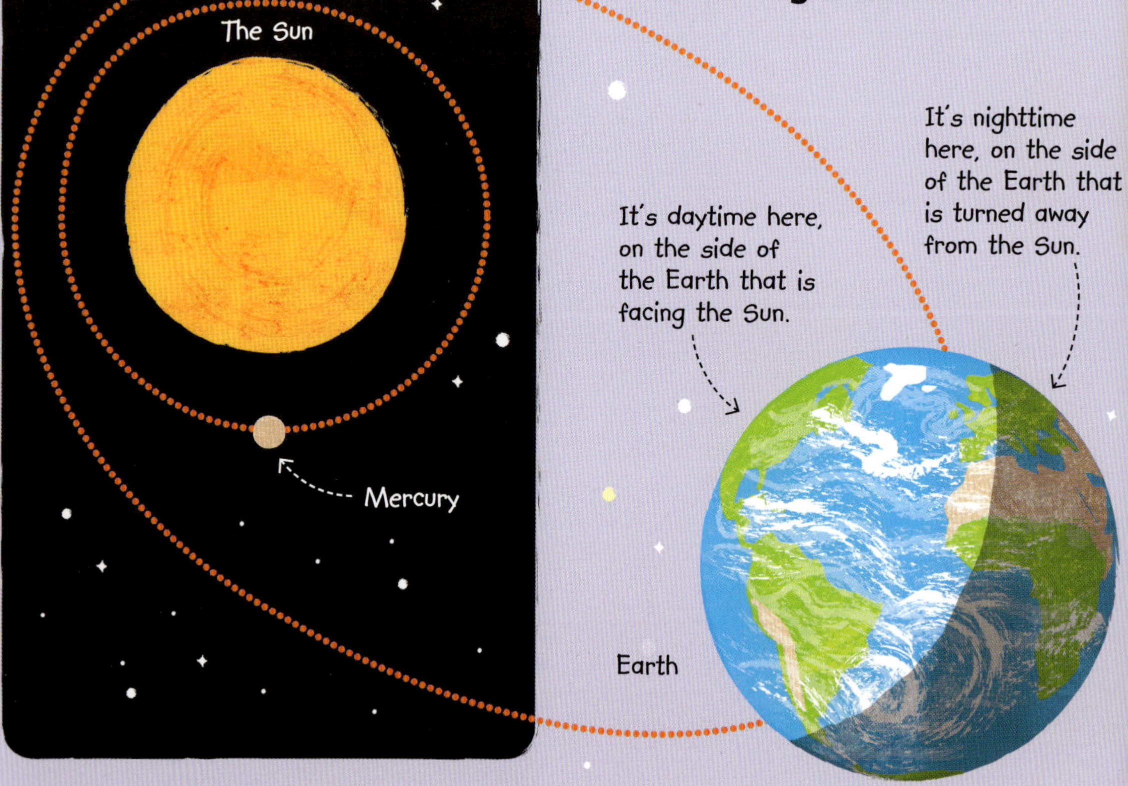

 Find out more about: orbiting (page 81); planets, the Sun (page 78)

Seasons

A season is a part of a year that has its own weather patterns and number of daylight hours.

The seasons happen because the Earth doesn't sit straight in space, but is tilted a little.

In summer and winter, one part of the Earth is tilted toward the Sun and the other is tilted away from it.

- **Spring** happens between winter and summer.

- **Summer** happens in the part of the Earth that is tilted toward the Sun.

- **Fall** happens between summer and winter.

- **Winter** happens in the part of the Earth that is tilted away from the Sun.

Find out more about: deciduous trees (page 27)

Scientific investigations

Investigating something means finding out as much as you can about it. Science is about finding out how the world works. You can do this by asking questions, doing tests and looking at what happens.

Questions

People ask questions when they want to know something. Questions often start with words such as 'Why,' 'Where,' 'How,' 'Which' and 'What.'

Scientific questions are about the way the world works.

Here are some questions that you could try to answer by doing a scientific investigation:

Why do some things float and other things sink?

Which activity makes your heart beat the fastest?

What type of soap makes the most lather?

Observations

Observations are the things you have seen and remembered of the world around you. These observations could give you ideas about the answer to the question you are investigating.

Before you investigate why some things float and others sink, you might have already observed that...

...a leaf floats in a pool of water...

...and a coin sinks when you throw it into a fountain.

These observations may give you the idea that only light things float. You will need to do a scientific investigation to see if your idea is right.

Sources

Before you do an investigation, you can look at books and websites to find out more about the thing you are investigating. The places where you find information are called sources.

To make sure the information is right, it's best to use more than one source.

Planning

Planning means deciding what to do and how to do it. You can draw or write about your plan for an investigation.

A plan for an investigation into floating might look like this.

Plan for investigation into floating

Put things of different weights into a bucket of water, one at a time.

Predictions

A prediction is a guess about what is going to happen. Your ideas, observations and sources can all help you predict what might happen in an investigation before you do it.

Thinking about what you already know, you might predict something like this will happen in an investigation into floating.

Predictions for floating investigation

I already know that a leaf floats, so anything lighter than a leaf will probably float too.

Leaf floats

Paperclip might float

I already know that coins sink, so anything heavicr that a coin will probably sink too.

Coin sinks

Apple might sink

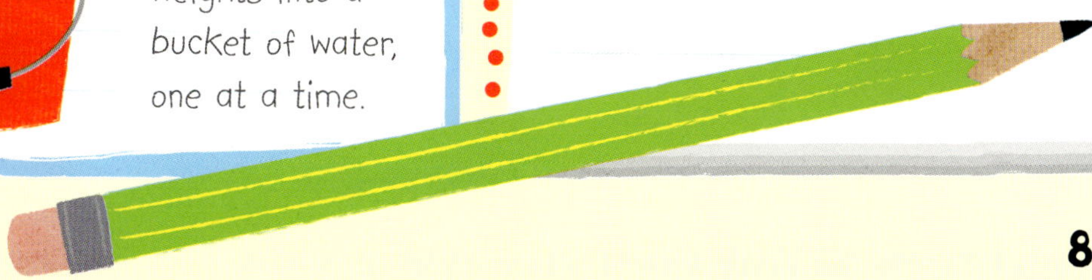

Equipment

Equipment is the things you need to do a job. Equipment for a scientific investigation is all the things you need to do the investigation.

This is the equipment you might use for an investigation into why things float.

Bucket of water to float things in

Weighing scale to find out how heavy or light the things you are testing are

Objects that you want to test, to see if they will sink or float

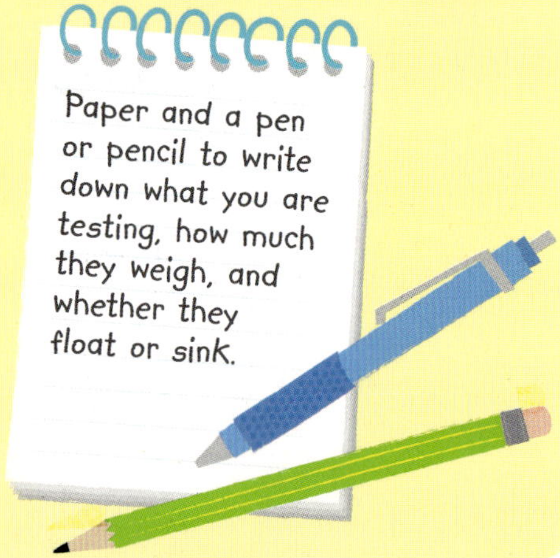

Fair tests

Tests are a way of seeing what happens when you try out an idea. Another name for a test is an **experiment**.

To be scientific, a test must be fair. This means that you should change no more than one thing every time you do the test. Everything else should stay the same.

For an investigation into why things float...

...the thing that you put in the water should change in each test...

Test 1: paperclip

Test 3: coin

Test 2: leaf

Test 4: apple

...but you should use the same liquid in the bucket for each experiment – water – and keep it at the same temperature.

 Find out more about: weighing scales (page 92)

Measuring

Measuring something means finding out how big, heavy, hot, or fast it is. You might need to measure the thing you are testing during a scientific investigation to find out if it is changing.

Length

Length is how far it is from one end of something to the other.

Measuring the length of this piece of yarn will tell you how long it is.

Height

Height is how far it is from the bottom of something to its top. It is also how far above the ground an object is.

Your height is the measurement from your feet to the top of your head.

Depth

Depth is the length of something measured from top to bottom.

The depth of water in a tank is its measurement from top to bottom.

Width

Width is the length of something measured from side to side.

The blue line shows the width of this box.

Distance

Distance is the amount of space between two things or places.

The distance the toy car moves is the amount of space between where it starts and where it stops.

Units of length

You can describe the size of any length using the words below. Each word stands for a different amount, known as a **unit**.

- **inches** (in)
- **feet** (ft)
1ft is the same as 12in
- **yards** (yd)
1yd is the same as 3ft
- **miles**
1 mile is the same as 1,760yds

1 inch line

The length of this guitar is around 1 yard.

In the UK and the USA, larger distances are also measured in units called **miles**.

Measuring length

Here are some of the tools you can use to measure length, height or distance:

- **Ruler** – a measuring stick used to draw and measure small, straight lines.

This ruler has inches marked on one side...

...and inches and fractions of inches on the back.

- **Tape measure** – a narrow strip of cloth or metal used to measure longer lengths.

The strip comes out of the case when you pull it.

- **Trundle wheel** – a wheel with a handle, which clicks every time it has been pushed one yard.

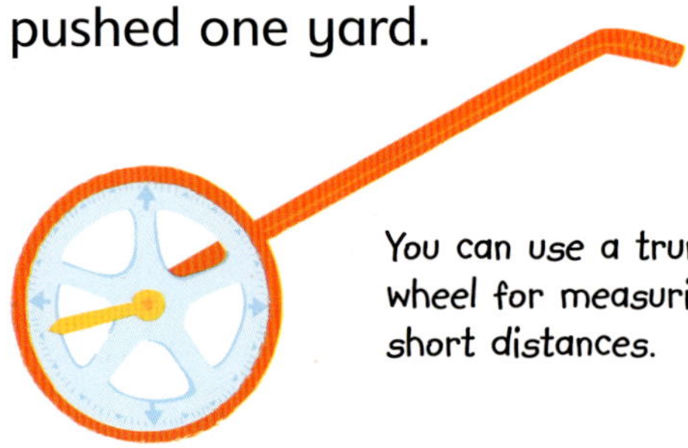

You can use a trundle wheel for measuring short distances.

 Find out more about: distance, height, length, measuring (page 89)

Weight

Weight is the measurement of how heavy something is. (Weight is often the everyday word for what scientists call **mass**.)

A sofa weighs more than a chair, so it is harder to lift.

Two things can be the same size but have different weights. That's because one of the things can be made of heavier materials than the other.

Rock is heavy, so this rock has more weight than...

...a bouncy plastic toy of the same size, which is full of air.

Units of weight

Here are some units you can use to talk about weight (what scientists call mass).

- **ounce** (oz)
- **pound** (lb)
  1lb is the same as 16oz
- **ton**
  1 ton is the same as 2,000lbs

A ping pong ball weighs about 1 ounce.

A pineapple weighs about 2 pounds.

A small car weighs around 1 ton.

Find out more about: materials (page 38); plastics (page 50)

Measuring weight

You can measure weight using different types of scales.

- To use **balancing scales**, put what you want to weigh on one side, and add weights to the other until the sides balance.

- To use **kitchen scales** like these, put what you want to weigh in the dish on top.

The pointer points to the weight on the scale.

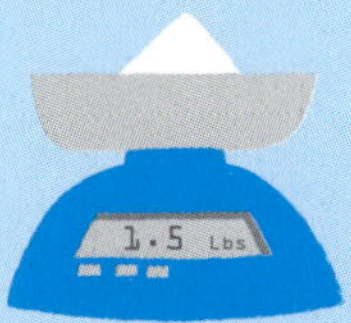

Electronic scales show the weight as a number.

- To use **bathroom scales**, put what you want to weigh on top.

You can stand on bathroom scales, and the pointer points to your weight.

Electronic scales show the weight as a number.

Temperature

Temperature is the measurement of how hot or cold something is.

Units of temperature

Temperature is measured in units called **degrees Fahrenheit**, which can be written as °F.

The temperature of a healthy person is 98.6°F.

When you are sick, your temperature is often higher than 98.6°F.

 Find out more about: measuring (page 89); units (page 90); weight (page 91)

Measuring temperature

You can measure the temperature of something using a **thermometer**.

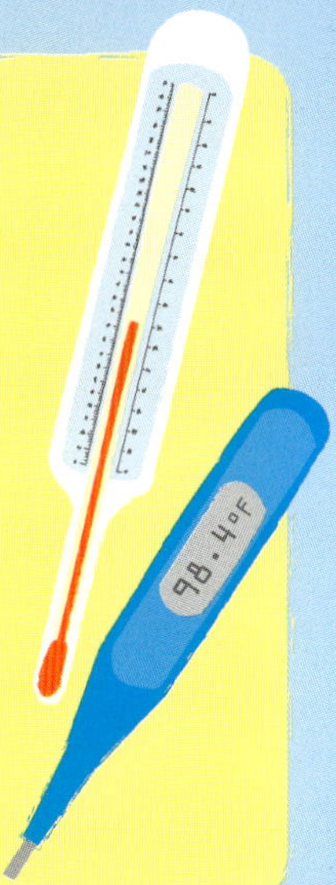

Some thermometers have colored liquid inside which moves up and down a scale to show the temperature. Other thermometers are digital.

Time

Time is a measurement of how long something takes to happen. Here are some units you can use to measure time.

- A **year** is the time it takes for the Earth to travel once around the Sun.
- There are 12 **months** in a year.
- A **day** is the time it takes the Earth to spin around once.
- You can split a day into 24 **hours**.
- There are 60 **minutes** in one hour.
- There are 60 **seconds** in one minute.

Measuring time

Here are some of the things you can use to measure time:

- A **clock** or **watch** shows hours, minutes and seconds.

This watch has hands: one moves a division every second, one moves a division every minute and one moves a division every hour.

Some clocks and watches don't have hands, but just show the time in numbers.

- A **calendar** shows the days and dates for each month of the year.

Find out more about: the Earth and the Sun (pages 84-85); liquids (page 51)

Volume

Volume is the amount of space something takes up.

This bucket has a big volume.

This cup has a small volume.

Units of volume

Here are some units you can use to talk about volume:

- **fluid ounces** (fl.oz)
- **pints** (pt)
  1 pint is the same as 16 fluid ounces
- **gallons** (gal)
  1 gallon is the same as 8 pints

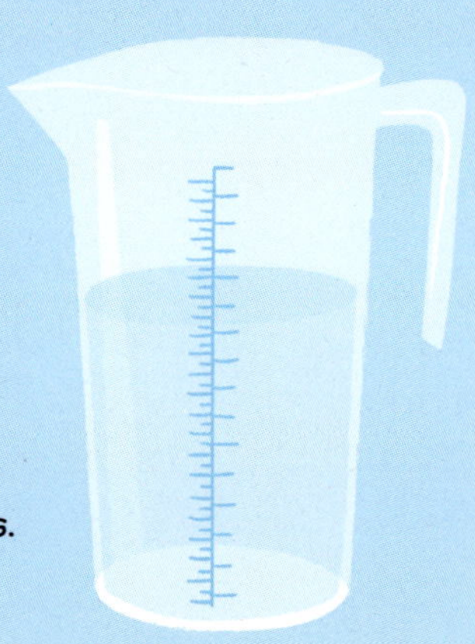

Measuring cups are see-through containers with measurements marked up the side, used for measuring liquids.

Measuring speed

Speed is the measurement of how quickly a thing moves.

To measure the speed that something is moving at, you need to find how far it travels in a certain time.

Units of speed

Here are some units you can use to talk about the speed of something:

- **yards per second** (yd/s)
  how many yards something can travel in one second
- **miles per hour** (mph)
  how many miles something can travel in an hour

A cheetah can run 75 miles in an hour.

A mouse can run about 4 yards in a second.

 Find out more about: hours (page 93); miles, units (page 90); measuring (page 89); speed (page 62)

Results

What happens in a scientific test or experiment is called its result or results. Here you can see some different ways to write down a set of results.

Making notes

While your investigation is going on, you can write down the results of the experiments as they are happening so you don't forget them.

These notes were written down during an investigation into floating.

Investigation into floating

FLOATED

Leaf

Paperclip

Apple

DIDN'T FLOAT

Coin

You can use your notes to show your results in a clearer way after your investigation has finished.

Tables

A table is a way of setting out your results in rows (going across) and columns (going down). A table is a good way of comparing the results of different tests in an investigation.

This table shows how far a toy car traveled along different surfaces.

	Distance traveled (in in)		
Surface	Test 1	Test 2	Test 3
Carpet	16	17	16
Wood	19	18	18
Glass	21	21	22

Find out more about: fair tests, experiments (page 88); surface (page 61)

Pictograms

A pictogram is a way to show amounts using pictures or symbols. Each symbol stands for an amount, and you can use part of a symbol to show a smaller amount.

This pictogram shows how many bubbles were made with one blow when different things were used as bubble wands.

This shows what each symbol stands for.

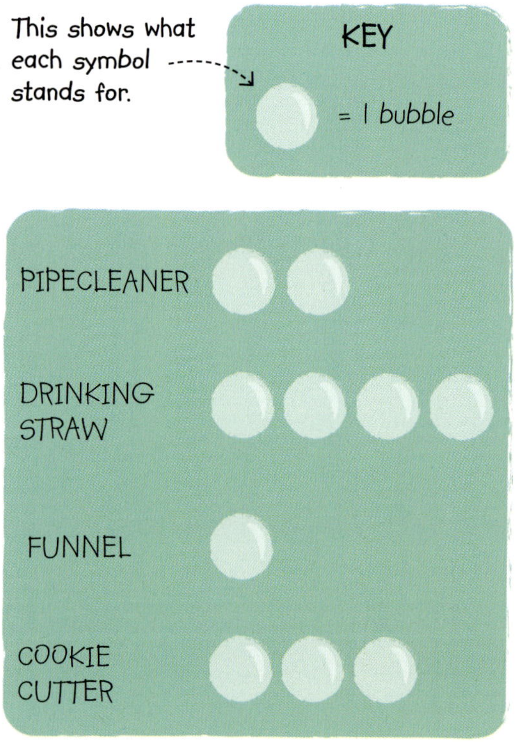

This pictogram shows that:
The pipecleaner made 2 bubbles.
The drinking straw made 4 bubbles.
The funnel made 1 bubble.
The cutter made 3 bubbles.

So you can easily see that the drinking straw made the most bubbles and the funnel made the fewest.

Bar charts

A bar chart is a way of showing different amounts using bars of different lengths.

Drawing a bar chart is a good way to compare the results of separate tests within one investigation.

This bar chart shows the results of an investigation into how long it took a child to move across the playground in different ways.

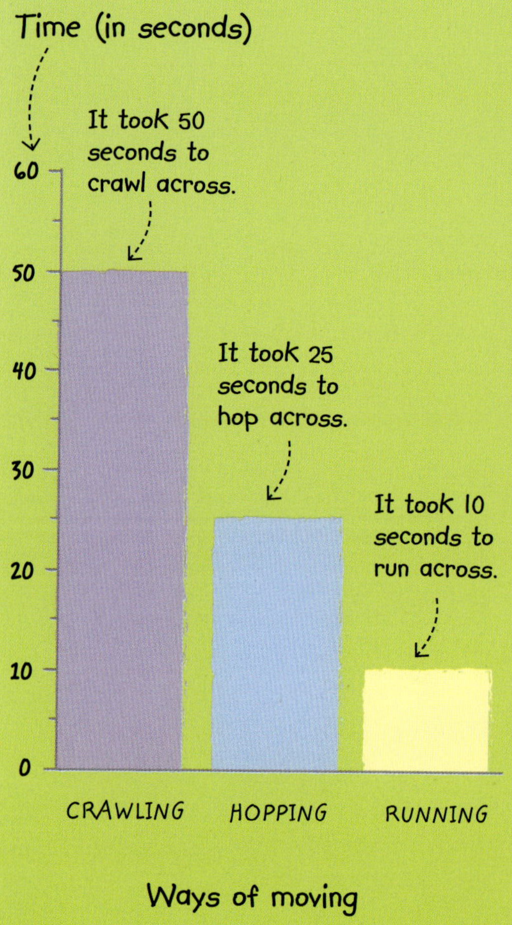

 Find out more about: length (page 89)

Looking at results

When you have set out the results of your investigation in a clear way, you can look at them to see if there are any patterns. You can also see if they match with what you predicted might happen.

In an investigation into floating, you might have predicted that the heavier something is, the more likely it is to sink.

Predictions for floating investigation

	FLOAT		SINK
	FLOAT		SINK

When you have the results, you can compare them to your predictions.

	Prediction	Result
	FLOAT	FLOAT
	FLOAT	FLOAT
	SINK	SINK
	SINK	FLOAT

Conclusions

A conclusion is how you explain the results of your investigation after you have looked at them.

Floating investigation conclusion

- Even though the apple is heavier than the coin, it didn't sink, as I predicted.

- Whether something floats or sinks isn't just about how heavy it is.

The results might fit with what you expected to happen. But if they don't, you might want to do more experiments to find out why not.

More floating experiments

- What something is made of might make it float. Try floating things that are made of different materials.

- The shape of a thing might make it float. Try floating things that are different shapes.

Find out more about: materials (page 38); predictions (page 87); results (page 95)

Word finder

t

u

Acknowledgements

Americanization by Carrie Armstrong and Kimberly Yates
Web researcher: Jacqueline Clark
With thanks to Phil Clarke

Photo credits

p20 cold virus © Sci-Comm Studios/Science Photo Library; p23 baby mouse © Steve Gschmeissner/ Science Photo Library; p23 baby © Jellyfish Pictures/Science Photo Library

First published in 2013 by Usborne Publishing Limited, 83-85 Saffron Hill, London EC1N 8RT, United Kingdom. usborne.com

First published in America 2013. This edition published 2026. AE.